A PINEAPPLE FOR THE KING

To

Lt. Col. P.D.S. Palmer, J.P., D.L.

A

PINEAPPLE

FOR THE KING

by

T.W.E. Roche

PHILLIMORE
London and Chichester

1971

Published by

PHILLIMORE & CO. LTD.
Shopwyke Hall, Chichester, Sussex, England

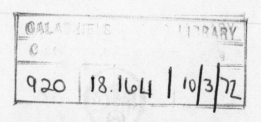

Text set by Phillimore in 11/12pt Press Roman
Printed on Brunel Antique Wove paper by
Redwood Press Limited, Trowbridge and London

CONTENTS

LIST OF PLATES

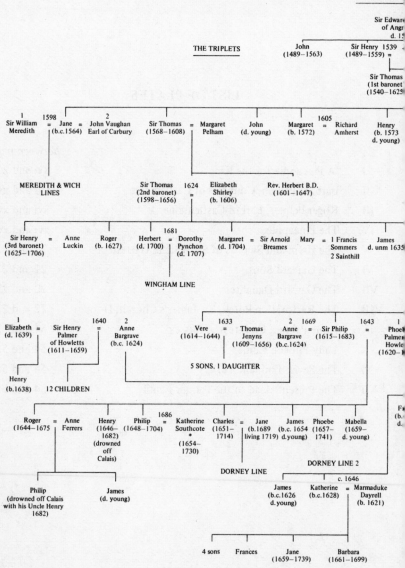

Sir Edward
of Angr
d. 15

THE TRIPLETS

John (1489–1563)	Sir Henry 1539 (1489–1559) =

Sir Thomas
(1st baronet
(1540–1625

1 Sir William Meredith	1598 = (b.c.1564)	Jane	=	2 John Vaughan Earl of Carbury	Sir Thomas (1568–1608)	=	Margaret Pelham	John (d. young)	Margaret (b. 1572)	1605 =	Richard Amherst	Henry (b. 1573 d. young)

MEREDITH & WICH
LINES

Sir Thomas (2nd baronet) (1598–1656)	1624 =	Elizabeth Shirley (b. 1606)	Rev. Herbert B.D. (1601–1647)

Sir Henry (3rd baronet) (1625–1706)	=	Anne Luckin	Roger (b. 1627)	Herbert (d. 1700)	1681 =	Dorothy Pynchon (d. 1707)	Margaret (d. 1704)	=	Sir Arnold Breames	Mary	=	1 Francis Sommers 2 Sainthill	James d. unm 1635

WINGHAM LINE

1 Elizabeth (d. 1639)	=	Sir Henry Palmer of Howletts (1611–1659)	1640 =	2 Anne Bargrave (b.c. 1624)	Vere (1614–1644)	1633 =	Thomas Jenyns (1609–1656)	2 Anne Bargrave (b.c.1624)	1669 =	Sir Philip (1615–1683)	1643 =	1 Phoe Palme Howle (1620–

Henry (b.1638)   12 CHILDREN   5 SONS, 1 DAUGHTER

Roger (1644–1675)	=	Anne Ferrers	Henry (1646–1682) (drowned off Calais)	Philip (1648–1704)	1686 =	Katherine Southcote * (1654–1730)	Charles (1651–1714)	=	Jane (b.1689 living 1719)	James (b.c. 1654 d.young)	Phoebe (1657–1741)	Mabella (1659– d. young)	F (b. d.

DORNEY LINE   DORNEY LINE 2

Philip (drowned off Calais with his Uncle Henry 1682)	James (d. young)		James (b.c.1626 d.young)	Katherine (b.c.1628)	c. 1646 =	Marmaduke Dayrell (b. 1621)

4 sons	Frances	Jane (1659–1739)	Barbara (1661–1699)

ARMS

Sir James Palmer of Dorney	Arms	= or, 2 Bars gules each charged with 3 trefoils slipped argent in chief a greyhound current sable
	Crest	= a demi-Panther guardant Argent semée of Hurts holding in the paws a sprig of holly fructed pr
Sir Henry Palmer of Howletts	Arms	= argent a chevron between 3 palmers' scrips sable, the tassels & buckles or
	Crest	= a dexter arm embowered in armour, couped at the elbow, holding in the hand a sword fracted

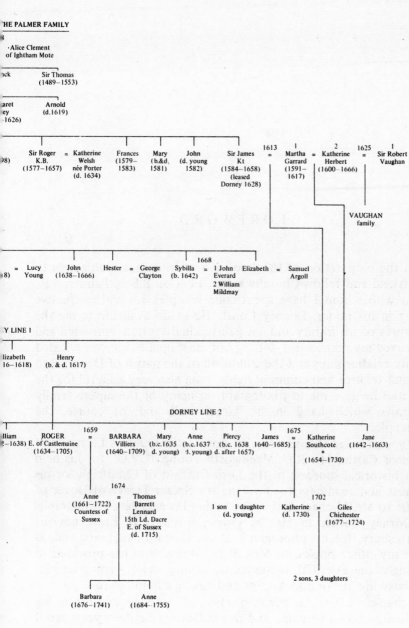

THE PALMER FAMILY

·Alice Clement
of Ightham Mote

Sir Thomas
(1489–1553)

Arnold
(d.1619)

| Sir Roger K.B. (1577–1657) | = | Katherine Welsh née Porter (d. 1634) | Frances (1579–1583) | Mary (b.&d. 1581) | John (d. young 1582) | Sir James Kt (1584–1658) (leased Dorney 1628) | 1613 = | Martha Garrard (1591–1617) | 2 Katherine Herbert (1600–1666) | 1625 = | 1 Sir Robert Vaughan |

VAUGHAN
family

| = | Lucy Young | John (1638–1666) | Hester | = | George Clayton | Sybilla (b. 1642) | 1668 = | 1 John Everard 2 William Mildmay | Elizabeth | = | Samuel Argoll |

Y LINE 1

| lizabeth 16–1618) | Henry (b. & d. 1617) |

DORNEY LINE 2

| lliam ?–1638) | ROGER E. of Castlemaine (1634–1705) | 1659 = | BARBARA Villiers (1640–1709) | Mary (b.c.1635 d. young) | Anne (b.c.1637 d. young) | Piercy (b.c. 1638 d. after 1657) | James 1640–1685) | 1675 = | Katherine Southcote * (1654–1730) | Jane (1642–1663) |

| 1674 |
| Anne (1661–1722) Countess of Sussex | = | Thomas Barrett Lennard 15th Ld. Dacre E. of Sussex (d. 1715) |

1 son 1 daughter
(d. young)

| 1702 |
| Katherine (d. 1730) | = | Giles Chichester (1677–1724) |

2 sons, 3 daughters

| Barbara (1676–1741) | Anne (1684–1755) |

y omission of greyhound 1645–1723)

FOREWORD

In the preparation of this book I owe an immeasurable debt to my friend and fellow-Churchwarden, Lt. Col. P.D.S. Palmer, J.P., D.L., with whom I have spent countless pleasant and instructive hours in his house, Dorney Court. He made available to me the treasures of his library and has painstakingly vetted, corrected and improved my manuscript, setting out most lucidly the complicated family relationships and the condition of the parish of Dorney and its land tenures and common rights. I am also very grateful for the facilities he gave me to photograph so many of the superb family portraits which hang in his Great Hall and, of course, the Pineapple.

My particular thanks are also due to the Queen's Librarian at Windsor Castle, Mr. R.C. Mackworth-Young, C.V.O., for his help with historical sources: to the Lord Clifford of Chudleigh for his interest and readiness to show me the Secret Treaty of Dover of 1670: to Mr. Michael Arthy, for taking his excellent photographs in Dorney Court: to Mr. W. Owen, formerly of Eton, now of Shaftesbury, for his photograph of the Garrard daughters: and, as with my other books, to Mrs. R.E. Green, who has provided so willingly the essential assistance of typing and re-typing despite her busy life at London Airport and having a home to run.

I thank my wife for her inspiration of this book and for having originally chosen to come and live in Dorney eighteen years ago. I must admit my great good fortune in being Churchwarden of St. James's, in having had access to its records going back to 1538 and to having acquired an intimate knowledge of the fabric and monuments of the Church so closely bound up with the history of the Palmers and their predecessors. I must also admit to some satisfaction in having been able to write this history of the family, for I think my old friend in Devon, the late Mrs. Mabel Stayner, would have been pleased to see it done, herself born a Palmer at Dorney Court; her Christian name recalls a 17th century Mabella who figures in the family tree and the latest stained-glass window in Dorney Church was installed five years ago in her memory.

Finally, I thank the Editor and Mr. D. Lingane of *The Windsor, Slough and Eton Express* for their interest and my publishers, Messrs. Phillimore, in particular Mr. Philip Harris, their Managing Director, and Mr. Noel Osborne, their Publications Manager, whose encouragement of my project and welcome to my wife and myself in their beautiful Shopwyke Hall near Chichester greatly cheered me on my way.

T.W.E. ROCHE

Dorney, Bucks, 1971

NOTES ON THE CALENDAR

In order to avoid the confusion which invariably arises over dates at this period, since France had adopted the Gregorian calendar from 1582 but Great Britain did not do so until 1752, I have throughout this book given the years in the modern style. Until 1752 the New Year in England was reckoned to start from March 25 and therefore such dates as '1 January 1660', sometimes shown '1660/1' would in our eyes relate to 1661. This is how they are shown here, though at the time they would not have been so written.

The adoption of Pope Gregory's new calendar by France, Italy, Spain and Portugal also led to a difference in ten days between the calendar as reckoned in those countries and in countries which still stick to the Julian Calendar. For example, differences appear in French and English sources regarding the dates of Minette's last visit to England and the signing of the Secret Treaty of Dover.

INTRODUCTION

Sir John Betjeman lamented the loss of the waving cornfields of Middlesex, engulfed by the tide of suburbia. Since he wrote that poem the tide has spread still further westwards and the built-up area now extends, with few breaks, out past London Airport and the industrial sprawl of Slough almost to the Thames, which separates Buckinghamshire from Berkshire. Almost—for just before the Thames is reached there is a final stretch of country which is still rural England.

The motorist on the M4 can just detect it, if he can take his eyes from the road long enough, but the most effective route to it lies past Eton College. Suddenly the bricks and mortar are left behind and ahead lies the broad sweep of Dorney Common where the cattle graze unhindered as their forebears have done since the 12th century. On the far side lies the village, still barely extended beyond its mediaeval shell: some of the houses are very old and even the petrol-pumps stand in front of a 16th century cottage!

One of the two inns, *The Palmer Arms,* stands in the Village Road, the greyhound and trefoils magnificently painted on its sign. At a curve in the road at the far end of the village is a junction, the major road bearing right past the secluded vicarage to the outlying hamlet of Lake End, where the second inn stands. This is *The Pineapple,* a vivid picture of the fruit swinging before it. The left turn at the junction is Court Lane, pursuing a sinuous course under great chestnut trees with arable land on the right and the woods bordering the manor estate on the left.

The traveller rounds the sharpest curve of all and there,

half-hidden from the lane, the gabled Tudor Dorney Court stands opposite the ancient church, whose most modern feature is a porch bearing the date 1661–significant enough, for it was added to commemorate the Restoration of King Charles II. The Palmer family, loyal adherents of the Stuarts, built that porch 35 years after they first came to Dorney Court. They live there still, after the passage of 340 years.

This book is an attempt to give them their rightful place in the century which saw them sacrifice so much for the Royalist cause and approach so near the Throne. Coming originally from Sussex and Kent, they were a race of country landowners whose normal preoccupation was the administration and improvement of their estates. Here and there in their history there were highlights, some happy, some tragic, beyond the compass of most contemporaries' experience. In the 15th century there were the triplets, born on three successive Sundays, a medical phenomenon of all time: in the 16th there was Sir Thomas alone of the family to suffer death by the headman's axe: in the 17th, alone in a family of dedicated Royalists, there was the Puritan divine, Herbert, who became Master of a Cambridge college. Outstanding however beyond all these is the story of Roger, avowed Papist, savant, sailor, ambassador, whose wife became the first and chief mistress of the most beloved of all English Kings.

On the wall of the Great Hall of Dorney Court hangs her portrait, the very one which Pepys so much regretted not being able to see when he called at Lely's studio. Below it and the many other Lelys and Knellers, stands on the high table a carved stone model of a pineapple with a plaque stating that it commemorates the first such fruit grown in England presented by Rose, gardener to Sir Philip Palmer, to King Charles II about the year 1665.

That is why I gave this book its title: the gift of the pineapple epitomized the attitude of the 17th-century Palmers to the House of Stuart, an absolute unswerving devotion which placed all things great and small at their service.

PROLOGUE

Dorney still bears the name the Saxons gave it, very little altered, the interpretation of which is 'the thorn island' or 'the island of the bumble-bees', according to which philological theory one supports. It was an island then and so remained for many centuries, surrounded in winter by the wide waters of the shallow, spreading Thames and in summer by marshes. Under the last Saxon King, Edward the Confessor, it was held by Eldred, a thane of Earl Morcar; *Domesday Book* described it as being held of Miles Crispin, the Lord of Wallingford, with ploughing land for twelve teams of oxen and woodland for 100 swine.[1] These woods were not in the low-lying vicinity of Dorney itself, but up in the hills above Burnham where there was neither river nor marsh but deep oak-wood and where the hamlet of Boveney also had pasturage, so that the names of Dorneywood and Boveneywood are perpetuated in the foothills of the Chilterns to this day. Boveney, a mile away, had a ford across the Thames and a wharf where barges could tie up to discharge cargoes for transport northwards overland and, near this point, in the 12th century, a chapel dedicated to St. Mary Magdalene was erected.

A simple Saxon church must have existed at Dorney, for some few of its stones, including the remains of a round-headed arch, are built into the present chancel wall, which also contains some Norman work. By the 12th century Dorney manor belonged to the Danvers family, and in their time the font was placed in the little church of St. James. No doubt it had a timber-roofed nave then and a floor at the present level of the font, with steps up to

XV

the chancel. It was the next century that saw the rapid expansion of this little place, when a shadow of international importance fell briefly across it.

In 1231 Richard, Earl of Cornwall, younger brother of King Henry III, secretly married Isabella, daughter of William the Marshal, without his brother's knowledge or consent, at Fawley in the Chilterns and brought her down to his manor of Cippenham for their honeymoon; here they narrowly escaped the full force of the King's displeasure, as Henry, fuming with rage in nearby Windsor Castle, would have had his brother seized and imprisioned but for the intercession of their sister, the Princess Eleanor.[2] In the event a reconciliation took place, but Cippenham and its neighbourhood always had a favoured place in Richard's memory, even after the death of Isabella Marshal and his remarriage and deflection to other greater places and weightier affairs of state.

He steadily amassed wealth and in 1257 was elected King of the Romans by a majority of the seven Electors of the Holy Roman Empire, being crowned in Aachen Cathedral with the silver crown of Germany, the only Englishman ever to aspire to the honour of Emperor. Unhappily for him, every time that imperial coronation in Rome seemed within his grasp, he was recalled to England to help his incompetent brother through a fresh crisis with the barons. So it was that, in 1264, he found himself not on his imperial throne but fighting with his brother and nephew, the Lord Edward, against Simon de Montfort at the Battle of Lewes. Captured there, he was removed first to the Tower of London and later to Kenilworth Castle, where he remained until released after the royalist victory at Evesham in 1265.[3] As part of his ransom Richard vowed, while in the hands of Simon de Montfort in the Tower, that if he were released he would build an Abbey on his lands. He had already done this very successfully once before, at Hayles in Gloucestershire, when he fulfilled a vow made in the stress of a storm at sea off the Scilly Isles. Now, on release from Kenilworth, he fulfilled his second vow and, seeking one of his manors on which to build the new Abbey, found what he sought in his lands of Burnham, close to Cippenham Palace where he had spent his honeymoon with Isabella Marshal 35 years before. The foundation charter was signed at Cippenham on 18 April 1266, in the presence of King Henry and the Lord Edward and numerous

I 'A PINEAPPLE FOR THE KING'
From the painting by Danckaerts now in Ham House
(reproduced by courtesy of Victoria and Albert Museum; photograph by Michael Arthy)

II BARBARA PALMER
Countess of Castlemaine, Duchess of Cleveland, from the painting by Sir Peter Lely at
Dorney Court
(reproduced by courtesy of Lt. Col. P.D.S. Palmer; photograph by Michael Arthy)

III ROGER PALMER
Earl of Castlemaine, from the painting by Sir Peter Lely in Dorney Court
(reproduced by courtesy of Lt. Col. P.D.S. Palmer; photography by Michael Arthy)

IV THE PINEAPPLE
Carved stone model on the high table of the Great Hall of Dorney Court
(reproduced by courtesy of Lt. Col. P.D.S. Palmer; photograph by Michael Arthy)

other dignitaries. From that moment forward a change came over the locality.[4]

Richard was unquestionably the richest man in England, and his money began to pour in to these small places. Dorney, whose revenues his brother granted him, received its first rector, Rowland, shortly after Richard's release in 1265; the advowson was placed in the hands of the Danvers family. The gift of the living remained with them until the year after the Earldom of Cornwall was made a Dukedom for the Black Prince; about 1368 it passed into the hands of the Abbess of Burnham, who retained it till the Reformation. 'The Convent of Burnham', wrote Lipscomb, 'having had appropriated to that House the Rectorial Estates subsequently presented to the living as a Vicarage'. This did not please the lords of Dorney and relations between them and the Abbess were at times distinctly strained; so much so that, after the Danvers' line had become extinct and the Newnhams had succeeded them, John Newnham, lord of Dorney, sent his men up to the Abbey and carried off by force the greater part of the tithes housed there, taking the Abbess's horses and carts back to Dorney as well for good measure.[5]

There followed a period when the manor changed hands a number of times. In 1430 it and 103 acres were conveyed to John Scot, from whom it passed by marriage to Richard Restwold. In 1504 The Restwolds sold it to Sir Robert Lytton for 500 marks but eight years later his family sold it to Richard Hyll, noted for his violent temper, who cut down the great oak on Dorney Common under which the local peasantry had been wont to disport themselves. It is to the Lyttons that we owe the construction, on the site close to the church of the beautiful half-timbered Dorney Court about the year 1510, as fair an example of an early Tudor manor house as any in the land. When the Lyttons sold the manor to the Hylls it was subject to the life interest of Thomas Lytton, but in 1513 the latter disposed of this for £40 and an annuity of £20, on condition that the use of certain rooms in the mansion should be reserved to him: this was the first recorded mention of Dorney Court. From the Hylls it passed in 1543, together with 1600 acres of land, to Sir William Garrard, haberdasher, Lord Mayor of London in 1555, for the sum of £600. He was succeeded by his son, also Sir William, in whose time the brick tower of Dorney church was built and the oldest of the present bells, dated 1582 and inscribed 'Blessed be the name of the Lorde' hung. It was this Sir William who was for a short while before his death a Gentleman of the Bedchamber to King James I. He died in 1607 and his magnificent memorial tomb, designed by Sir John Kedermister, who had married Maria Garrard at Dorney on 5 September 1597, stands in the chapel which bears his family's name. This chapel, rebuilt in the late 16th and early 17th centuries to house the Garrard memorial tomb and family vault below, was originally a 14th century structure. In the 15th century a fine fresco of the Annunciation was painted on either side of the doorway leading into it from the north side of the chancel, showing the Angel Gabriel on the left and the Virgin on the right.

Sir William's wife, Lady Elizabeth, was also the daughter of a former Lord Mayor of London. They had fifteen children, as the monument shows and one of their younger daughters, Martha, married Sir James Palmer, a younger son of the house of Palmer of Wingham in Kent, in 1613.

The origin of the Palmers is quoted by the 'Palmer pedigree' as follows:

'The Palmers of Sussex were acknowledged by the whole County one of their ancient families before the Conquest though the name came from the Holy War: for Palmer signifies Pilgrim because they carried (as Camden says) a Palm when they returned from Jerusalem. The name usually had no particles before it yet some heretofore after the custom of the Normans (who often added *de* or *le* to theirs) added them also to this; for we find in *Villare Contiarum* p.322 William de Palmer and in the *Monasticon* John le Palmer in the time of Hen 3. All our adventures in the Holy War (as Fuller and others have it) were called Pilgrims or Palmers and therefore several brave champions after the most Christian Expedition retained this devout appellation. So that there have been about 60 considerable families at a time in England of this very surname differing in their Arms and in no way related but by marriage.'

This then is the story of the Palmer family who were flourishing landowners in Sussex in the reign of Edward I. Their business was the art of estate management which they have carried out with some degree of success until the present day. Although owning substantial acreages they never approached the size of the really great families of England and never held any of the great offices of state. They were mainly concerned with local government, although they produced several Members of Parliament. The younger sons, with their own way to make in life, were usually soldiers or went in for trade; they included one distinguished divine and for at least 150 years up to 1683 they had the honour of serving in the King's household, mostly as gentlemen of the Privy Chamber.

For instance, when Henry VII came to the throne the head of the family was Sir Edward Palmer of Angmering, Sussex. He had two younger brothers, the first being Robert Palmer, citizen and mercer of London, who at the Dissolution of the Monasteries bought the Manor of Parham, Sussex, for £1225.6s.5d. and died there on 13 May 1554. His son, Sir Thomas, pulled down the old house and Robert Palmer's great grandson, another Sir Thomas, then a child of two and a half, was allowed to lay the foundation stone of the present magnificent mansion of Parham on 28 January 1577.

This last Sir Thomas went to sea and was with two of the greatest admirals of Devon, Sir Francis Drake and Sir John Hawkins, in their expedition to Porto Rico. At the age of twenty-two he commanded a ship at the taking of Cadiz in 1596, where he was knighted by the Earl of Essex. About 1601 he sold Parham to Sir Thomas Bishop, Knight and Baronet (who also bought Angmering from another Palmer in 1616). Then in 1605 he went with the Earl of Nottingham into Spain and died of smallpox at Valladolid. His father had married Elizabeth Verney and thus came into possession of Fairfield, another magnificent house with a fine estate, situated near Stogursey in West Somerset. Early in James I's reign the Parham Palmer children moved there too and their descendants through the female line still live there today.

Sir Edward Palmer married Alice Clement, co-heiress of Ightham Mote in Kent and sister to Sir Richard Clement of the King's Bedchamber. In those days of large families the Palmers were exceptional in having three children whose birth was so remarkable that they have remained unique in medical science to

this day. In the summer of 1489 Lady Alice produced the famous
Palmer triplets who were born not within hours or even a day of
each other, but one on each of three successive Sundays; the
eldest, John, appeared on Whit Sunday, 7 June, the second,
Henry, on Sunday, 14 June and the youngest, Thomas, on
Sunday, 21 June. The story is well documented and the tradition
has survived in the Palmer family for nearly 500 years, while the
baby clothes of the triplets are still in the possession of a
descendant of the house—Lord St. Audries, of Fairfield,
Stogursey, Somerset, to whom they were handed down from
Peregrine Palmer, the last of the Somerset branch of the family,
who died in 1762.

The triplets thus so strangely born lived to what was in those
days a considerable age and all distinguished themselves in their
country's service. John, as the eldest, succeeded to the family
lands at Angmering and was twice High Sheriff of Sussex and
Surrey during the reign of Henry VIII. He died in the fifth year of
Elizabeth I at the age of seventy-three, having made two
advantageous marriages.

The youngest, Thomas, was a professional soldier, who was
much in favour with Henry VIII. He saw service at Tournai in
1515, was appointed Gentleman of the Privy Chamber to the King
four years later, went with him to the Field of the Cloth of Gold
in 1520 and was knighted by the King at Calais on 10 November
1532. Two years later he was appointed Knight Porter of Calais
and held the post for seven years. He was taken prisoner by the
French at Guisnes and had to ransom himself, which he could well
do, having received the possessions of no less than four major
religious houses at the Dissolution of the Monasteries. However,
though he basked in the King's favour and was used by Henry on
certain secret missions because of his proven boldness and valour,
in March 1541 his fortunes underwent a sudden change. Recalled
from France ostensibly to secure a special pension, he was in fact
brought back to get him into the King's power and on arrival was
thrown into the Tower and deprived of his post of Knight Porter
of Calais.

However, he seems to have re-established himself, for by the
first year of Edward VI's reign he was joint commander of the
English forces at Haddington and had distinguished himself

particularly:

> 'a recruit of about one hundred foot and three hundred horse led by Sir Robert Bowes and Sir Thomas Palmer was so fatally intercepted [by the Franco-Scottish force] that they were almost to a man killed' but as for Bowes and Palmer, 'yet they lost no heart.'

Sir Thomas was once again captured by the French but later ransomed. He amassed sufficient wealth to start the construction of a fine town dwelling in the Strand, but did not complete it before his death. It later became known as Exeter House, being enlarged and embellished by William Cecil, Queen Elizabeth's Treasurer.

As a soldier he was brilliant, as a politician not so able; it was his dabbling in politics which led to his downfall. He became involved first with the Lord Protector Somerset and was again confined in the Tower along with him but apparently was brought secretly to the young King and gave evidence against the Duke, with the result that he was called as chief witness at Somerset's trial. It was said that Sir Thomas was chiefly responsible for ruining him, but there were intrigues afoot which made it doubtful where the blame lay. Defence witnesses were not called—their evidence was read—and Somerset was beheaded on 22 January 1552, many onlookers dipping their handkerchiefs in his blood as a memento of a man widely admired.

If Sir Thomas was guilty of betraying the Duke, Nemesis was at hand. As a Protestant he espoused the cause of Lady Jane Grey, with whose uncle, Northumberland, he had naturally been allied as an opponent of Somerset; and on 19 August 1553, six weeks after Mary Tudor's accession, he was tried as 'a bold and most unscrupulous partisan of the Duke's.' It may also be that he was condemned not so much because he was party to Lady Jane's succession as because Somerset had been beheaded and his family wanted revenge. Palmer was bold to the last; he scornfully told Mary's Commissioners that they were as much traitors as he and worse, and his speech from the scaffold on Tower Hill was long remembered as a cheerful and courageous oration.

> 'Good morning to you all, good people'

he cried, smiling;

> 'ye come hither to see me die and marry, I will tell ye what news I have. I have seen more in yonder terrible place'

—and he pointed to the Tower—

'than ever I have seen before throughout all the realms that I have wandered in; for I have seen God, I have seen the world and I have seen myself; and when I beheld my life, I saw nothing but slime and clay, full of corruption; I saw the world nothing else but vanity, and all the pleasures and treasures there of nought worth; I saw God omnipotent, His power infinite, His mercy incomprehensible, and when I saw this, I most humbly submitted myself unto Him, beseeching Him of mercy and pardon and I trust he has forgiven me; He called me once or twice before, but I would not turn to Him, but even now by this sharp kind of death He has called me unto Him. I trust the wings of His mercy will spread over me and save me; and I do confess before you all, Christ to be the very Son of God the Father, born of the Virgin Mary, which came into the world to fulfil the law for us and to bear our offences on His back, and suffered His passion for our redemption, by the which I trust to be saved.'[8]

Turning to the headsmen, he said,

'Come on good fellow, art thou he that must do the deed? I forgive thee with all my heart.'

Then he knelt down, and laid his head on the block saying

'I will see how meet the block is for my neck; I pray thee strike me not yet, for I have a few prayers to say, and that done, strike in God's name, good leave hast thou'.

'His prayers ended', ran the contemporary account, 'and desiring eche man to praie for him he layed down his head agayn, and so the hangman toke yt from him at one stroke.'[9] Thus died, valiant to the last, at the age of no less than sixty-six, the youngest of the Palmer triplets and the first of the three to die.

The second of the triplets, Henry, married Jane, daughter of Sir Richard Windebanck, captain of Calais, then still an English possession. Her mother, Lady Margaret, was of Welsh extraction, being the daughter of Gruffydd ap Harry. Henry was a professional soldier and later succeeded his father-in-law in office at Calais and also as Bailiff of Guisnes in Picardy and Master of the Ordinance. This was in 1539, and five years later Henry had his arm broken at the siege of Boulogne. Along with his brother he was knighted by Henry VIII who, in recognition of his services, granted him the former College of Secular Canons in Wingham in Kent on the Dissolution of the Monasteries. In 1553 Edward VI sold to Sir Henry the house of the Provost of Wingham and all the tithes that were paid to the Church and an acre of glebe for £519.11s.4d., subject to a payment of £20 per annum to a Vicar.

Thus it was that Sir Henry Palmer came into possession of those gracious oid buildings which were to form the nucleus of the manor that was to be the cradle of generations of Palmers. Wingham is one of the most charming of the many picturesque villages lying to the east of Canterbury, in a particularly fertile part of Kent. The great church had been the collegiate foundation of the secular canons, whose houses are now the inns and cottages of the village. Sir Henry would still recognise the church as we see it today; its essential feature is light—lightness in the great porch, lit by five windows, in the nave and aisles, supported by six great chestnut beams, in the ancient chancel with its Norman sedilia and curiously carved *miserere* stalls.

Arrested by order of Queen Mary in 1553, along with his brother Sir Thomas, Sir Henry was soon freed and returned to Picardy. He was wounded in an expedition from Guisnes against the French in December 1558, shortly after Calais fell and England lost her last possession on the mainland of Europe. He returned to England to retire at Wingham, but was not destined to enjoy it for long, as he died the following year as the result of his wound.

His eldest son, Thomas, was left a Ward at about seventeen and came of age in the fourth year of Elizabeth's reign. In 1562 he married Margaret Poley of Badley, Suffolk, granddaughter of Lord Wentworth, Henry VIII's Treasurer and Comptroller of the Household. The couple entertained Queen Bess at Wingham in September 1573, when she was on her way from Sandwich to Canterbury. Thomas became High Sheriff of Kent in 1595 and a Gentleman of the Privy Chamber to James I, who created him a baronet on 29 June 1621, and he was buried at Wingham. His wife died in August 1626, in her eighty-third year. In 1627 their eldest surviving son, Sir Roger Palmer, K.B., erected a splendid monument to his parents on the north wall of the chancel of Wingham Church: it was moved to its present site in the North, or Brooke, Chapel when the church was restored in 1874—5. It bears a strong resemblance to the Garrard monument at Dorney but on it we see Sir Thomas and Lady Margaret lying side by side, not kneeling facing each other. Their epitaph tells us

> 'The Threads of their lives were evenly spun. They lived in concord and died in peace, beloved of their neighbours, lamented of their friends, honoured by their children and missed by the poor, for whose sake they never brake up house for sixty years.'

Of their eleven children, six died in infancy, as was all too common in the 16th century. Of the survivors, Jane married first Sir William Meredith of Stanslie, Denbighshire and secondly John Vaughan, Earl of Carbury: her picture as a child, stiff in her Tudor ruff, hangs in the Great Hall at Dorney Court. Another daughter, Margaret, born in 1572, was married at the comparatively late age of thirty-nine to Richard Amhurst of Bayhall and Pembury, Sussex, Serjeant-at-Law. The eldest son, Sir Thomas, was educated at St. John's, Cambridge and Gray's Inn: he married Margaret Pelham of Michelham, Sussex, and was knighted on 11 May 1603. He died in his father's lifetime at the age of forty and was buried at Wingham on 10 September 1608: he left a son, another Thomas, then aged ten, who later matriculated from St. John's. He married Elizabeth, daughter and co-heiress of Sir John Shirley of Isfield, Sussex and it was he who, on the death of his grandfather, Sir Thomas, in 1625, succeeded to the baronetcy and to the Wingham estate.

As we have seen, the eldest surviving son of Sir Thomas and Lady Margaret was Sir Roger Palmer, Knight of the Bath. It is said of him that Lord Bacon, being acquainted with him at Gray's Inn, brought him to Court where his good qualities soon got him friends for

> 'he could vault and ride the great horse very well. He was also a master in vocal and instrumental music. He understood Spanish and Italian accurately, but in dancing he was so excellent that few, if any, in his time came near him especially in galliards and high dancing, which was then most in request.'

He was presented in 1600 by Lord Effingham to the Queen who presently entertained him as a servant: but she dying in 1603 he was made Cup Bearer to Prince Henry and later to Charles, both as Prince and King. His father was a Gentleman of the Privy Chamber of James I and his younger brother James of the Bedchamber. About 1617 his high spirits got the better of him and at a Ball before the King he broke the great tendon of his right leg in capering. At Charles I's coronation the King made him a Knight of the Bath, then Master of the Household and, lastly, Cofferer.

Their youngest son, James, as we have seen, married Martha Garrard of Dorney in 1613 which gave him his first contact with the place. By her he had four children, but only Philip, his son and heir, and his daughter Vere survived. Unfortunately Martha died, after only four years' married life, at the early age of twenty-six on 1 July 1617, giving birth to a son, Henry. It may be that the two surviving children were then brought up at Dorney by Lady Garrard, their grandmother, for James, their father, had perforce to spend most of his life at Court. A continuing career there or in the Army would probably have been his portion had it not been for the unexpected events of the year 1625, both on the national and the family level, events which were to lead directly to the youngest son of the family of Wingham becoming the first Palmer of Dorney.

I

THE MAN OF KENT

EARLY IN 1625 James Palmer fell sick of an ague at the same time as King James I and 'made trial of the same plaister prescribed by the Duke and Duchess of Buckingham'. It cured James, in his own estimation, but the King was not so fortunate and died from his illness on 27 March.[1]

The new King, Charles I, already had a full complement of Gentlemen of the Bedchamber but he continued to grant James the usual pension of £500 per annum. As to his domestic problems, James's mother-in-law, Lady Garrard, had died on 7 December 1624 and he felt he ought to marry again and provide a home for his children.

He had been a widower for eight years and was now forty-one. In 1625 he married Katherine, sixteen years his junior, widow of Sir Robert Vaughan of Llwydiarth and Llangedwyn Hall, in Montgomery. She had one son and one daughter by her former husband and was the daughter of Sir William Herbert, K.B., created first Baron Powis of Powis Castle, Montgomeryshire, the great 'Castell Coch' or 'Red Castle' which had been a famous Marcher fortress since the Middle Ages. Her mother was of another famous line, the Lady Eleanor Piercy, daughter of Henry, 8th Earl of Northumberland. Katherine brought with her a substantial landed property in Wales, so that James had already become a landowner a short time before he came to Dorney.

There had been bitter and complex family quarrels among the Garrards after the death of Sir William, and since the eldest son had little interest in or capability for the management of a large

1

estate they decided to sell the property. So, in about early February 1626 Sir Roger Palmer, K.B., bought it and on the 13th of that month released and quit-claimed to others the interests in Dorney and elsewhere of the late Sir William Garrard. His younger brother James had evidently conceived a great liking for the place which had been his first wife's home and it seems likely that Roger allowed him to reside in Dorney Court from 1626 onward. On 3 July 1628 Roger leased Dorney to James and the latter bought it from him at some later date.

So the Palmers came to Dorney. In those days any newcomer to this agricultural area was treated as a stranger for at least fifty years. How then did Sir James, who was knighted by King Charles I in 1629, this man of Kent and youngest son, come to be accepted in Dorney and what manner of man was he?

James was baptized at Wingham on 29 January 1584. He was well versed in *belles lettres* (or 'BELLE LITTERE' as the Pedigree has it) and in all things befitting a courtier. He had, as we have seen, been a Gentleman of the Bedchamber of James I. He was a miniaturist of considerable distinction and there are at Dorney such paintings by him of his first wife Martha and his mother-in-law, Lady Garrard, which at one time were attributed to Isaac Oliver. Another of his miniatures, dated 1623, was sold at Sotheby's in November, 1969 for over £4,000, an indication of the value placed on his works in modern times. Because James understood pictures admirably, Charles I made him Keeper of his Privy Closet, where he was responsible for the King's pictures and helped him build up his collection.

None of these talents however suggests that Sir James could be a great country landowner able to manage estates both at Dorney and in Wales. Nevertheless, with his inherited instincts and the help of those of his wife, he was to be outstandingly successful. The condition of Dorney then, if not its extent, differs so greatly from that of today that it is worth considering what the organisation and population of the Parish was like 340 years ago.

Sir James was fortunate in inheriting an experienced Vicar, the Rev. Thomas Baker, who had been at Dorney since 1596 in the days of Sir William Garrard. The Vicar, with his glebe and his tithes, his Parish meeting, Parish Clerk and two Churchwardens, was a man of great importance and his influence touched every aspect of the way of life of his parishioners, for good or ill.

The Manor of Dorney with Boveney consisted of nearly 1600 acres, of which the major part was common fields: there were as well Dorney and Lake End Commons, as now: 52 acres of small enclosures, 46 acres of demesne land immediately attached to the manor house while 39 acres were accounted for by the River Thames and 11 acres by roads. In addition there were about 418 acres at Dorney Wood and Burnham Beeches and some 22 acres elsewhere—very similar to what it had been in the Middle Ages.[2]

The framework of the 17th-century village can be detected today because field boundaries, where they existed, were hedges on top of banks with a ditch on one side. The common fields were fenced against the common meadow and both were fenced against the Common itself.

Arable cultivation rotated round the common fields year by year in a three-year cycle, so that in any one year some would be cropped and the remainder left fallow. These fields, which had no internal fences, were divided into shotts or veres, which were in turn sub-divided into strips of one rood, half an acre or one or more acres. Holdings of strips were all intermingled, so that each person had some good and some bad land. There were thirteen such fields divided into 81 shotts or veres, sub-divided into 889 strips. For instance, one large farmer had 173 acres in 104 strips dispersed in 56 shotts or veres in 13 fields. There were sixteen freeholders, twenty-three tenants of the Lord of the Manor and Church and Chapel lands. The Common meadow was similarly divided into unfenced shotts or veres with 137 strips plus 3 swarths. Once the hay crop was taken the meadow was used for pasture. There were horse ploughs, hand labour and a few farm wagons.

Because of the complicated system of land tenure the farming economy (arable, cattle, horses, sheep, hogs or geese) was controlled by decisions made by the Jury of the Manor Courts, held before the Steward of the Manor. They also appointed the Bailiff, four overseers and a hayward to ensure that agreed decisions were carried out. The first such Court held in Sir James's time was on 12 January 1630, when, amongst other things, his brother-in-law Sir John Kedermister, architect of the Garrard monument, was presented for encroaching seven acres on Lake

End Common, he was ordered to remove it on pain of a £20 fine.

An added difficulty was that the greater part of the parish was flooded almost every year by the River Thames, as it had been since the days when the Saxons dubbed it 'the thorn island'. Long experience therefore ensured that properties were only built on sites above flood level. So we find Dorney Church, Boveney Chapel, Dorney Court, Boveney Court, Dorney Vicarage with its 17th-century extensions, several farmhouses of about eight rooms and numerous pairs of cottages with two or more rooms each and wattle and daub walls—what the West country would term 'cob'—built just out of reach of the encroaching waters.

There were open fireplaces and spits, home-made bread, well water and earth closets. Most of the inhabitants were illiterate. Life revolved round the horse, so the smithy and the wheeler's yard were places of importance. There were also other village handicrafts such as the hurdle maker, chairmaker, thatcher, carpenter, and so on. There was little money about and payments were often made in kind or by so many hours' or days' labour. Dorney and Boveney were a community working together and largely self sufficient. Many of the families had been there for generations.

In 1631 a second bell was hung in Dorney Church inscribed 'Prayse the Lorde'. The following year the Rev. Thomas Baker, Vicar for the past thirty-six years, died and in 1633 Sir James presented the Rev. William Flood to the living. This event must have almost coincided with the marriage of Sir James's daughter Vere to Thomas, son of Sir John Jenyns of Hertfordshire, which took place at St. Martin-in-the-Fields on 8 May 1633. Vere's husband's family was related to that of the famous Sarah, Duchess of Marlborough, whose future husband, John Churchill, was also to figure in a different connection in this story.

Sir James and Lady Katherine Palmer were determined to beautify their ancient church of St. James the Less, and the following year their master carpenter, Henry Fellow, installed the splendid symmetrical minstrel's gallery at the western end under the tower arch. It is a cunningly contrived piece of work, neatly fitted into the available space above the Norman font, 500 years its senior: the builders of old understood acoustics so well that they placed the gallery where the slightest sound from it is carried clearly right up into the chancel. Its maker's name and date, written 'Henry Felo 1634' are still clearly visible.

Henry Fellow had evidently lived in Dorney for some time. He is first mentioned in the Court Rolls at the Manor Court of Dame Elizabeth Garrard, widow, held on 2 December 1616, where it is shown that he had bought of John Garrard two tenements and divers lands in the common fields. His stint was four cow and two horse commons, so he must have had about sixteen acres.

This gallery's construction coincided with the birth of a remarkable man. On 3 September 1634, Lady Katherine gave birth to a son, who was baptized Roger by the Vicar, the Rev. William Flood, at the font in Dorney Church the following day. The register of births in Dorney Church reads: '[1634] Roger son of Sir James Palmer Kt and of Dame Katherine his wife was baptized ye 4th September.' Roger was the first surviving Palmer son born after his parents moved to Dorney and was to become, partly through reflected glory, partly through his own efforts, the most famous of them all in the 17th century. As the eldest son of his father's second wife he would never, in the ordinary course of events, have succeeded to the Dorney estates: that honour was reserved for his eldest half-brother, Philip, the son of Sir James by Martha Garrard. But Dame Fortune can play some sardonic tricks.

Meanwhile Sir James had been appointed by King Charles I a Gentleman Usher of the Privy Chamber. This office carried with it a particular personal responsibility to the Sovereign. The duty was

'to wait on the King's person within doors and without, so long as His Majesty is on foot: and when the King eats in the Privy-Chamber, they wait at the Table and bring him his meat. They also wait at the reception of Ambassadors: and every night two of them lie in the King's Privy-Chamber. A Gentleman of the Privy-Chamber, by the King's command only, without any written commission, is sufficient to arrest any Peer of England, as Cardinal Wolsey acknowledged. They wear always cloak and sword (whereas the Grooms of the Privy-Chamber do not).'[3]

Thus the Lord of Dorney was brought into close contact with the second of the Stuart Kings of England, a charming but stubborn and unbending man. Charles's marriage to Henrietta Maria, daughter of the French King Henry of Navarre, had started off badly, due largely to the influence of the Duke of

Buckingham, but after the latter's murder in 1628, a great change came over Charles. No longer disapproving and crushing to his sparkling little French wife, he fell deeply in love with her. After five years of marriage she gave birth to a son, christened Charles, on 29 May 1630, followed next year by a daughter, Mary, two years later, in 1633, by another son, James, and in 1635 by another daughter, Elizabeth. Thus Sir James's period of office under the King coincided with the happiest period of his ill-starred reign, when Miss C.V. Wedgwood in her book, *The King's Peace* described him as 'The Happiest King in Christendom'. In 1637 Sir James Palmer was appointed Governor of the Mortlake Tapestry Works and the following year found himself advanced to the honour of Deputy Chancellor of the Order of the Garter.

To revert to Dorney: when he became Lord of the Manor common rights were held according to an ordinance of 11 June 1626 which stated

> 'The rent of 5/- by the year to keep a cow, or sow, or bacon hog and a youngling, that is to say a beast under the age of three years, a goose and a gander.'

Those paying higher rents could keep more beasts, horses or sheep according to scale.

A revoluntionary change occurred at the Manor Court of 8 November 1637, when control by size of rent was abandoned and the concept of a fixed number of animals based on a sliding scale according to the acreage held with a cottage or house was introduced. These rights were appurtentant and they form the origin of those now registered under the Commons Registration Act of 1965.

The wording in the Court Roll is:

> 'Order made for the waste, commons and common fields of Dorney and Boveney by common consent of the Lord of the Manor and tenants of all the manors there at a Court holden 8th November 1637.
>
> 1. *Imprimis* it is ordered that no lands held several in inclosure shall be allowed any common in the wastes and commons and fields aforesaid . . .
>
> 2 *Item,* that the stint or rate for cattle, horses and beasts shall to each man for his house and land commonable which he has in his own occupation, that is to say, to every cottage,

though having no land in the field, one cow and one youngling bullock: and to him that has three acres of land with his messuage is further allowed one neat beast and no more; and to him that has five acres is allowed for further increase one horse beast and no more: and afterwards the increase of every five acres shall increase one horse and no more: provided that no man shall exceed the number of nine horses, whatsoever the quantity of his land shall be.'

So eleven years after coming to Dorney the Man of Kent obtained the consent of its inhabitants to a major change in entitlement to grazing on the Common which for 300 years has served satisfactorily as the basis for using the great green 'waste'.

Locally things looked fair, but nationally they were heading for disaster. While Lady Katherine Palmer produced two daughters, Frances and Mary, and the Queen a son, Henry, born in 1639 and created Duke of Gloucester, the growing opposition to the King's absolutism hastened the storm. Trouble brewed in England and in Scotland; open revolt flared in Ireland: Charles sacrificed his faithful servant Strafford in May, 1641 and Archbishop Laud some years after him, the latter blessing the former from his window in the Tower as he was led to his execution.

Under the impetus of a Buckinghamshire gentleman, Hampden, his colleague Pym and the formidable Oliver Cromwell, the tide surged on to civil war and on 22 August 1642, King Charles raised the Royal Standard at Nottingham and the most terrible inter-necine strife since the Wars of the Roses was unleashed upon England.

II

CONFLAGRATION
(1642–1657)

ON THE outbreak of war Sir James moved his family up to his estates in Montgomeryshire, leaving Dorney in the hands of his Steward. There in Wales he raised a troop of horse at his own expense, maintaining it in the Royalist service throughout the campaign. Debts due to him from the Crown amounted to no less than £7,718.18s.10d., according to his estimation on 25 May 1651—an enormous sum 300 years ago. Parliament having sequestered his estates, he compounded for a very substantial sum of money. All this resulted in a disastrous lack of capital, which was to affect the family adversely for over 100 years. In fact, unlike other families who had divided allegiance, all the Palmers of Wingham, Fairfield and Dorney, with only one notable exception, supported the Royalist cause and all those who were of an age to bear arms did so. All three branches suffered, like Sir James, heavy financial loss. His son by Martha Garrard, Philip, became an officer in the Royalist Army and rose rapidly in rank: the Palmer pedigree says of him, 'He was Colonel for Charles in the great Rebellion and behaved well in many engagements.' A year after the Civil War broke out, in 1643, Philip, then aged twenty-eight, married Phoebe Palmer, aged twenty-three, daughter of Sir Henry Palmer of Howletts, Kent, Vice-Admiral of the Narrow Seas: father and daughter's portraits also hang in the Great Hall at Dorney, a photograph of that of Phoebe, painted by Janssen in 1632, appearing on another page.

Meanwhile the daughter of another Royalist house was growing up: she was to have a great influence on the future of Roger

8

Palmer and his family. The great family of Villiers, Dukes of Buckingham, had long stood in high favour at Court: George Villiers was created Duke on 18 May 1623 and his cousin Sir Howard who married Barbara, daughter of Sir John St. John and niece of Oliver St. John, first Viscount Grandison of Limerick, Ireland, had a son by her, William Villiers, later to become second Viscount Grandison. In 1639 he married Mary, aged fourteen, third daughter of Paul Viscount Bayning. A year later she gave birth to a baby daughter, who was baptized Barbara at St. Margaret's, Westminster. She was two at the outbreak of the Civil War and only a year later, on 24 July 1643, her father, a Royalist Officer, was wounded at the siege of Bristol. Less than a month afterwards he died of his wounds at Oxford at the early age of thirty, where, years later, his daughter was to erect a memorial to him. His gallantry and charm earned him a tribute from no less discerning a man than Lord Chancellor Clarendon.

This miserable conflict flailed about the country for four long years in the first instance: broadly it could be said that the King's strengths first lay in the north and west, Parliament's in the south-east and East Anglia. There were of course odd exceptions: Exeter, for example, fell briefly into Parliamentary hands in 1643, to fall to Royalist forces under Prince Maurice on 4 September. As Cromwell's military organisation in the east improved, Queen Henrietta Maria came westwards seeking refuge and found it in Exeter, where in Bedford House, the town dwelling of the Russells, Dukes of Bedford, she gave birth on 16 June 1644 to the Princess Henrietta.

Charles I came to see his baby daughter in July and the same month his forces, under Prince Rupert of the Rhine, suffered a crushing defeat at the hands of the Roundheads at Marston Moor. It was far enough away from Exeter, but there were other Parliamentary forces nearer, under the Earl of Essex. Soon the Queen was forced to flee from the city, leaving her baby behind in the care of Lady Dalkeith. Cromwell, suspecting the Queen's intention was to embark for France, sent a fleet into Torbay to prevent her. Henrietta Maria contrived to escape into Cornwall and embark safely for France from Falmouth, whose Pendennis Castle was destined to be the very last fortress to hold out for the King. Meanwhile Essex's forces came to Lostwithiel in hot pursuit of

her; finding some Royalists in the church tower, they tried to
blow it up with gunpowder and, failing, led a horse into the
church and 'christened' it 'Charles' at the font to insult the King.
Royalist reinforcements under the King were at hand, however,
and Essex suffered a crushing defeat. Charles went back to Exeter
in September to see his baby daughter again; for a while it looked
as if the Royalist fortunes were in the ascendency.

In the east, however, Cromwell was busy assembling his New
Model Army and soon areas loyal to the King were being forced to
surrender. Meanwhile Sir James Palmer was active in the area
round Montgomery: on 5 September 1645, he wrote to Prince
Rupert, telling him of the state of the war in Wales and in
particular of the 'Red' Castle of Powis. Perhaps as a result of this
letter Charles I visited Powis and Llanfyllin on the 21st of the
same month.[1]

The same year Sir James attained his supreme honour as
Chancellor of the Most Noble Order of the Garter on the death of
Sir Thomas Roe. At the same time he differenced his arms from
those of the Wingham Palmers by omitting the greyhound, which
had been part of them for centuries. The greyhound eventually
returned to the arms of the Palmers of Dorney in 1723, when the
baronetcy came to them on the failure of the Wingham line.

That same year came the Royalist defeat at Naseby and in the
following twelve months the King's fortunes disintegrated,
resistance petering out till only Salcombe and Pendennis Castles
held out for Charles, then only Pendennis, until it too finally
surrendered. 1646 was a year of disaster for the Royalist cause and
Charles saw the last of his baby daughter, who was taken over to
France to join her mother after two years' separation.

After the Articles of Oxford of 1646, Sir James Palmer was able
to return to Dorney but did not do so for another year; he found
it plundered by the Roundhead soldiery, all his plate, jewellery,
pictures and furniture gone. They had even torn down panelling in
the hopes of finding money hidden behind it.[1] To an artist like Sir
James this must have been a particuarly bitter blow, but it was
accepted as part of the sacrifice for the Royalist cause. Despite the
disaster and misery, life must go on: Sir James had come back to
Dorney in December 1647, bringing with him his young son,
Roger, who was sent to Eton College the following year at the age

of fourteen.

1648 saw a brief rekindling of resistance, known as 'the second Civil War'. This in itself encouraged fanatical Puritans to suppress the last vestiges of royal strength: overweening men sat in judgement on their King and, to the horror of much of the country and especially of such devoted adherents as the Palmers, Charles Stuart was executed outside his own Palace of Whitehall on the afternoon of 30 January 1649. When his headless corpse was laid to rest in St. George's Chapel, Windsor Castle, Parliamentary soldiers surrounded the few permitted mourners for fear of demonstrations.

Now the heavy hand of Cromwell fell upon all those places which had supported the King, among them Dorney, whose Vicar, William Flood, was deprived of his living. Other members of the Palmer family had fared equally ill, save only one. This was Herbert, the second son of Sir Thomas Palmer of Wingham. He had been baptized there on 29 March 1601, matriculated as a fellow commoner at St. John's, Cambridge, in Lent 1616, became a B.A. in 1619 and an M.A. in 1622. The following year he was elected a Fellow of Queen's and in 1631 received his Bachelor of Divinity degree. He was appointed a University preacher a year later and for fifteen years was Vicar of Ashwell, Hertfordshire, some fifteen miles from Cambridge. During the second year of the Civil War, 1643, he became a lecturer at Westminster Abbey and President of Queen's, Cambridge, in 1644, being appointed Master when it and other Cambridge colleges were 'purged' by the Parliamentarians.

A renowned Cathecist, he became a member of the Westminster Assembly when Parliament and the Scottish Presbyterians were purging the Churches. During this Westminster Assembly Herbert Palmer, together with three other divines, made one great plea for toleration, but this was rejected. It seems therefore that, convinced Puritan though he was, he did not suffer from the blind bigotry of so many of his persuasion. What High Churchmen thought of him is however epitomized by Archbishop Laud, who at his trial claimed in his defence that he had shown great tolerance, citing as an example the preferment he had given to Herbert Palmer, whose opinions he abominated. It is said that, just before Laud's execution on 10 January 1645, Herbert offered to come and pray with him, but the Archbishop thought him a mere hypocrite and declined the offer.

Cleveland in his poems referred to Herbert as 'Rumpled Palmer' by virtue of his crookedness of body. To the rest of his staunch Royalist family his beliefs must have been anathema, but Herbert did not have long to enjoy the ascendency of the Parliamentary factions, for he died unmarried in 1647.

Very different was the story of Peregrine Palmer, the heir to Fairfield, Somerset. He was four years younger than Herbert and was his contemporary at Cambridge, albeit at Christ's, not St. John's. After being admitted to Gray's Inn on 14 March 1625, he went as a volunteer to the Palatinate in the Thirty Years' War and later became an officer in the Swedish army, taking part in the great Battle of Lutzen in 1632, in which the famous King of Sweden, Gustavus Adolphus, was killed. When war broke out between England and Scotland, Peregrine served as a volunteer in the Earl of Essex's regiment and received a captain's commission, but was later dismissed the service on being accused of complicity in the plot to bring up the Army to aid Parliament. That this was untrue is shown by his faithful service to the Royalist cause directly the Royal Standard was raised in Nottingham. Peregrine served King Charles as a Major (September 1643), Lt. Colonel (November 1643) and Colonel of Horse (1644), being present at the battles of Edgehill, Marston Moor, Cropredy Bridge and Naseby and also at the battle of Langport, at which he served as a volunteer. After the defeat of the Royalist armies he retired to Flanders, there to await the King's commands to serve him as and when required.

For Royalist resistance was not entirely over by any means. King Charles landed in Scotland in 1651 and invaded England till his ultimate defeat at the Battle of Worcester. Thereafter, a fugitive with a price on his head, he escaped detection solely through the courage and loyalty of English country people, gentry, clergy, craftsmen, labourers. Reaching Dorset, he hoped to embark at Charmouth, but the plan failed: he was recognised and the Roundhead forces, it is said, clattered by along the Bridport road while he hid in the branches of an oak tree. Their preoccupation with their expedition to suppress the Island of Jersey probably led to their failure to find him. Miraculously he evaded them all, riding through the lonely interior of Wiltshire and Hampshire till at last he came down to the sea near Chichester and found the ship to convey him to safety—and exile.

There were other risings in his name—the Earl of Glencarne in Scotland, to whom Charles sent Peregrine Palmer as his agent, and several in England for which he had a similar assignment. After the abortive rising of the Cornishman, Penruddock, in 1655, Cromwell clapped on the regional government of his hated Major Generals who drastically tightened the screw—a model for Nazi *Gauleiter* three centuries later.

Roger Palmer left Eton at the age of seventeen and a half and matriculated as a commoner at King's College, Cambridge at Easter, 1652. He remained there for four years, coming to London on 29 October 1656 on admission to the Inner Temple 'to learn something of the law'. His arrival in London closely followed that of a particuarly beautiful girl. This was Barbara Villiers, then aged fifteen and a half:

> 'being left destitute both of a father and a future when she first
> came to London, she appeared in a very plain country dress:
> but this was soon altered into the gaiety and mode of the
> Town: she became the object of divers young gentlemens'
> affections.'[3]

Barbara's mother, after five years' widowhood, had married again in 1648 but she did not need to change her name as her new husband, to whom she gave her hand in the church of St. Bartholomew-the-Less in London, was another Villiers, Charles, Earl of Anglesea, a cousin of Barbara's father and, like her mother, then twenty-three years of age.

Among the 'divers young gentlemen' whom Barbara's vivid beauty attracted was Philip Stanhope, a handsome young widower who had just returned from two years' absence abroad on succeeding to his grandfather's estates and honours as Earl of Chesterfield. Barbara met him in September 1656, at her stepfather's town house and from letters which passed between them in 1657 when she was not quite seventeen, it was clear that she and Chesterfield had become lovers. They evidently did not contemplate marriage.

'My Lord'
she wrote to him

'the joy I had of being with you the last night had made me doe nothing but dream of you, and my life is never pleasant to mee but when I am with you or talking of you: yet the discourses of the world must make mee a little more circumspect: though I desire you not to come tomorrow, but to stay till the party and come to town, I will not faile to meet you on Saturday morning, till when I remain your humble servant.'

Some time during the autumn of 1656, however, Roger Palmer was introduced to Barbara, also at her stepfather's town house and became infatuated with her beauty: unlike Chesterfield he wanted to marry her and his courtship met with such success that Roger went down to Dorney and told his father. However old Sir James 'having strong surmises of the misfortunes that would attend this match, used all the arguments that parental affection could suggest to dissuade his son from it.' Indeed, he is reported to have said, 'If you persist in marrying that woman, I predict that you will live to be the most miserable man in the world'. As Roger was entirely dependent on his father for an allowance and as Barbara had no dowry, they had no option but to postpone their marriage at least until Roger's education was complete. In the meantime her affection for Roger did not interrupt her affair with the Earl of Chesterfield. The coming year, 1658, was, however like 1625, to prove a watershed in Palmer family fortunes.

III

INFATUATION
(1657–1659)

A PERIOD of great change was now coming upon both the country and the Palmers. First, on 15 March 1658, Sir James Palmer died and was buried in the vault at Dorney; now that his father had died and he had inherited his Welsh estates Roger Palmer encountered no further obstacles to his marriage plans. Meanwhile Philip Palmer, then aged forty-three, became Lord of Dorney in his father's stead. Another Palmer had been buried in the vault there a few months before Sir James—his elder brother, Sir Roger, Knight of the Bath, who had died on 8 October 1657; though a Palmer of Wingham, it was he who had bought Dorney from the Garrards in the first place and leased it to his younger brother James, so it was by no means strange that he should wish to be buried there.

Meanwhile Philip Palmer's half-brother Roger's infatuation with the delectable Barbara remained as intense as ever. Now approaching eighteen, she must have been an extraordinarily attractive girl, with her vivid complexion, profusion of dark auburn hair, wit, charm and intelligence, the former sharpened by contact with London minds. Roger had little to offer—his father had been paying for his studies at the Inner Temple at the time of his death and he had not as yet any settled career—but then Barbara had no dowry. However, on 3 April 1658 Sir James's will was proved and on 31 May 1659 probate was granted. Roger waited till he obtained his inheritance and then proposed marriage to Barbara, who accepted him. Their wedding took place on 14 April 1659, at St. Gregory's Church by St. Paul's, Roger being then twenty-four

15

and Barbara eighteen and a half.

So Roger had the most beautiful wife in London and Barbara financial security, despite the inroads into the Palmer family fortune made by the Civil War and the activities of Cromwell's Government. As yet the Crown was in exile in Flanders, but stirrings of liberty in Great Britain were apparent. On 3 September 1658, Oliver Cromwell, the Lord Protector, died; his son Richard—'Tumbledown Dick'—a sorry and quite inadequate replacement, succeeded him. Cromwell, having sensed the public mood of disgust, had purged the Army of some of its worst fanatics: the first cracks were showing in the granitic monolith of Puritan power.

It was fortunate for England that it was so, for it enabled the most moderate and far-sighted of Cromwell's generals to become the strongest of all, to acquire power steadily, shrewdly and patiently, his methods in keeping with his nature. For this man was George Monk, a typical North Devon squire from Potheridge by Torrington, a man who kept his own counsel to such a degree that his critics denounced him as surly and taciturn.[1] In a period of intense danger, of numerous plots, of back-biting, when a false step could lead to the block or the gallows and cauldron, a man who could keep his mouth shut was fortunate both for himself and his country. Aided in the background by his wife, the former Miss Clarges, variously described as a virago and—by Samuel Pepys—'always dowdy', Monk won over the more rational officers in the Army. When the time was ripe he marched south from his headquarters in Scotland, while the remains of Parliament in London haggled and trembled at his approach; wise in his generation he kept them guessing to the last and once in the capital put up a smoke-screen by marching into the City. While London wondered whether he was their liberator or just another Puritan dictator, North Devon took North Cornwall into his confidence and laid his plans to recall the King.

The man he trusted was Sir John Grenville, son of the famous Royalist general Sir Bevil, nephew of Sir Richard, 'the King's General in the West, and great-grandson of that other Sir Richard, Queen Elizabeth's great Admiral who had died when his *Revenge* took on fifty-three Spanish ships single-handed off the Azores in 1593. He could scarcely have found a more trusty emissary: the two West countrymen understood one another and kept each other's confidence. Charles, meanwhile, had left Brussels by a night ride in the nick of time before the Spanish Governor of Flanders prevented him—part of Louis XIV's devious politics—and found a new refuge in Breda in the United Provinces of the Netherlands. Still as poor as a church mouse, his luck was beginning to turn at last.

Monk's influence led to the free election of the so-called Convention Parliament early the following year, consisting mainly of moderate Roundheads and some traditional Royalists. Among the latter was a young man whose family's record of loyalty to the Crown was irreproachable—Roger Palmer.

It was a pity his political success was not matched by his private life. His beautiful wife, whose very steps he doted upon, continued her liaison with the Earl of Chesterfield and from her letters to him it is evident that Roger showed his displeasure, for Barbara referred scornfully to 'Mounser's' (Monsieur's) objections. Too late he must have realized where his blind infatuation had led him and recalled perhaps the words of old Sir James. Soon after their marriage Barbara had fallen very ill with smallpox, but fortunately she recovered and equally fortunately for her it did not in any way impair her vivid beauty.

IV

RESTORATION
(1659–1660)

THE YEAR 1660 was extremely eventful, both for the country at large and for the Palmer family, witnessing an event unparalleled in the history of the monarchy after our disastrous and only experiment with republican government. The winter and spring of 1659/60 were the scene of intense diplomatic activity. The quiet Devonian, General Monk, carefully tested the pulse of public opinion and then sent his emissaries to Holland to invite the King to return.

On 17 January Pepys, on his way to Kensington 'understood how that my Lord Chesterfield had killed another gentleman about half an hour before and was fled.'[1] Barbara's lover had in fact engaged in a duel with a young student of the Middle Temple named Francis Woolley, the son of a former chaplain of King Charles I, the subject of the quarrel being

'a mare of eighteen pounds price . . . They fought on the backside of Mr. Colby's house at Kensington, where the Earl and he had several passes. The Earl wounded him in two places and would fain then have ended, but the stubbornness and pride of heart of Mr. Woolley would not give over, and the next pass was killed on the spot. The Earl fled to Chelsea and there took water and escaped. The jury found it chance-medley . . .'[2]

As we would say nowadays, accidental death, but the Earl was not to know this; the Lord Protector's strict laws against duelling were still in force and so Chesterfield wisely fled to France and thence to Holland, where he presented himself, a suppliant, at Breda and Charles readily granted him a royal pardon.

18

On 16 March Pepys went

> 'to Westminster Hall, where I heard how the Parliament had this day dissolved themselves, and did pass very cheerfully through the Hall, and the Speaker without his mace. The whole Hall was joyful thereat, as well as themselves, and now they began to talk loud of the King. To-night I am told that yesterday, about five o'clock in the afternoon, one came with a ladder to the Great Exchange and wiped with a brush the inscription that was on King Charles, and that there was a great bonfire made in the Exchange and people called out "God bless King Charles the Second!" '[3]

But matters were still uncertain; twelve days later, when Pepys was on board the *Swiftsure,* where

> 'at night there was a gentleman very well bred, his name was Bames, going for Flushing, who spoke French and Latin very well, brought by direction from Captain Clerke hither, as a prisoner, because he called out of the vessel that he went in "Where is your King, we have done our business, Vive Le Roi!" He confessed himself a Cavalier at heart, and that he and his whole family had fought for the King. . . . My Lord had a great kindness for him, but did not think it safe to release him, though he had supper in the master's cabin'[4]

—thus uncertain was the position still.

April saw the fate of England in the balance. Pepys was heading westwards down the channel, when

> 'at dinner-time Mr. Cooke came back from London with a packet which caused my Lord to be full of thoughts all day and at night he bid me privately to get two commissions ready, one for Captain Robert Blake to be Captain of the *Worcester,* in the room of Captain Dekings, an Anabaptist, and one that had witnessed a great deal of discontent with the present proceedings. The other for Captain Coppin to come out of that into the *Newbury* in the room of Blake, whereby I do perceive that General Monk do resolve to make a thorough change, to make way for the King.'[5]

On 25 April the Convention Parliament met. Lord Sandwich, on hearing that the Earl of Manchester was chosen Speaker of the House of Lords, Sir Harbottle Grimston of the Commons and Sir Henry Yelverton, Pepys's old schoolfellow, member for

Northamptonshire, told him 'how he did believe that the Cavaliers now have the upper hand of the Presbyterians.'[6] Indeed, he could have added that a very loyal Cavalier family now represented Windsor, for on that day Roger Palmer took his seat as burgess for the royal borough which lies so near to Dorney.

Events now started to move with great rapidity. On 3 May Lord Sandwich showed Pepys the King's offer of grace to those that would come to him within forty days, and on the quarter-deck the papers were read and put to the vote and 'the seamen did all of them cry out "God bless King Charles! " with the greatest joy imaginable.'[7] On the 7th Lord Sandwich went round the fleet to see what alterations there must be to the arms and the flags, and two days later Pepys penned a letter for him to the King declaring the loyalty of the Fleet; 12 May, after anchoring 'over against Dover Castle', Sandwich 'had high debate with the Vice and Rear-Admiral whether it was safe to go and not stay for the Commissioners' and so weighed anchor and sailed for Scheveningen to go and fetch the King home from exile.

On Sunday, 13 May Pepys watched tailors and painters at work on the quarter-deck, 'cutting out some pieces of yellow cloth in the fashion of a crown and C.R. and put it upon a fine sheet, and that into the flag instead of the States' arms.'[8] On the 14th they could see The Hague clearly and dropped anchor off Scheveningen. Nine days of hectic activity followed; on the 20th the States of Holland gave a farewell banquet in honour of Charles at The Hague and three days later he embarked in the flagship *Naseby*. With all the flag-sewing and repainting the Admirals had left this ship with the name of a royalist defeat; Charles rapidly noticed this and had her re-christened *Charles;* other ships with Commonwealth names likewise received happier appellations. On that afternoon Charles, walking the quarter-deck fell to musing and telling the story of his escape after the Battle of Worcester, his privations, the loyalty of the English country folk he encountered, his crossing to Fécamp and his arrival, a pauper, in Rouen.

Now, however, the days of the fugitive were over. On 25 May, after a seaman's breakfast of pease and pork, the King went ashore at Dover in the Admiral's barge and there, ahead of the Mayor and Corporation and the wildly enthusiastic townsfolk, came his faithful General Monk to greet him. Monk, who had been acclaimed as a hero all the way down from London, had lain the night at Canterbury but risen at three o'clock on being told the Fleet was in sight. He modestly asserted that he was 'but the Morning Star· to usher in a Rising Sun' and journeyed down to Dover, where on the shingle he knelt before his royal master, who raised him and led him under the canopy prepared for him to speak with him a short while alone.

After a brief visit to Dover, Charles hastened on to Canterbury, where he was horrified to see the Cathedral looking so neglected and derelict. He stayed at St. Augustine's and received many diplomats and notables; on the following morning he made Monk a Knight of the Garter. The King wrote that night to his sister, the Princess Henrietta,

'My head is so prodigiously dazed by the acclamation of the people and by quantities of business that I know not whether I am writing sense or no.'[9]

On Sunday 27 May after service in the Cathedral, he set out for Rochester and London.

'Never',

wrote Dr. Grumble,

'were seen such numbers of people of all Degrees and Conditions lining the road from Dover to London; many women and children came many miles and placed themselves upon hillocks on the way, and many men upon trees (like Zaccheus) to see the blessed sight, and all with the greatest joy, blessing God that they had lived to see the day of his Majestie's Restortation, and were ready to sing their *Nunc Dimittis* even willing to depart in peace now that their eyes had seen the Salvation of their Country.'

Among those who followed in his wake was Pepys—who had brought Charles's favourite spaniel ashore at Dover. The company lay next night at Rochester and started again early in the morning of Thursday, 29 May 1660, Charles's thirtieth birthday, for the climax of it all. After reviewing the Army at Blackheath, Charles exchanged his coach for a horse and at half-past four in the afternoon rode over London Bridge and into the City of London amid scenes of wild rejoicing. So he turned westwards down the Strand where, among thousands of others, John Evelyn was watching him as he passed, smiling and brandishing his hat, the emotion of his joy-starved subjects almost too great to be borne.

So Charles II passed the scene of his father's execution and came into the Palace of Whitehall, where Parliament awaited him with loyal addresses. Too tired, after his nineteen-hour day, to make the last pilgrimage to Westminster Abbey, he made his Thanksgiving in private in the Presence Chamber. Then, when all the loyalists and place-seekers had left him, he remarked drily to his entourage that it was his own fault he had stayed away so long, as he had met nobody in England who did not protest that he had always desired his return; and so, tired but extremely happy, as the last event of this tremendous and never-to-be-forgotten day, he slipped into Barbara Palmer's arms.

V THE HELM AND SWORDS OF SIR WILLIAM GARRARD
and the pastels of Sir Philip Palmer and his son, Henry Palmer, in Dorney Court
(reproduced by courtesy of Lt. Col. P.D.S. Palmer; photograph by Michael Arthy)

VI THE GARRARD SONS
from the tomb in Dorney Church
(photograph by W. Owen)

VII THE GARRARD DAUGHTERS
from the tomb in Dorney Church
(photograph by W. Owen)

VIII THE RESTORATION PORCH, ST. JAMES'S CHURCH, DORNEY
Added in 1661
(*photograph by courtesy of* The Windsor, Slough and Eton Express)

V

THE KING'S MISTRESS
(1660–1663)

ANDREW MARVELL, that bitter opponent of the Stuarts, summed up sardonically what had happened at Charles's Restoration:

'In slashed doublet he came ashore
And dubbed poor Palmer's wife his royal whore'

It has been said that Roger and Barbara went to Brussels in 1659 and that they returned with Charles in May, but this seems incompatible with Roger having taken his seat as Burgess for Windsor in the Convention Parliament on 25 April; moreover, Pepys makes no mention of Mrs. Palmer having sailed with the fleet from Scheveningen to Dover, which he obviously would have done had she been there. Nor does Evelyn—or for that matter any other eye-witness of Charles's triumphal re-entry to London— mention her as having been in his train. The inference is that she was already in London and the King met her and fell for her at the banquet given at Whitehall that evening. Where they spent the night has again been the source of dispute—some Victorian writers having averred that the King slipped out of the Royal Palace and went to her at Sir Samuel Morland's house in Lambeth. None of the contemporaries suggest this, however, and it seems improbable— it was far more likely that the monarch summoned her to him in the Royal Palace. Barbara apparently conceived that night, for, writing from Paris to the King many years later in 1678, she declared that Anne, who was born just a week less than nine months after Restoration night, was the King's child.

Barbara and Roger were now residing at a house at the north

23

end of the west side of King Street, Westminster, next door to the Earl of Sandwich, Pepys's patron, and the latter had an obliging housekeeper, Mrs. Sarah, who was able to supply Pepys with all the latest gossip. Pepys had begun his *Diary* on New Year's Day at the age of 27, and as a connoisseur of womankind, had an eye to Barbara Palmer. He notes on 13 July that His Majesty, accompanied by his brother, James, Duke of York, attended a party 'with much musique' at a certain house in King Street—'the King and Dukes with Madam Palmer, a pretty woman that they had a fancy to, to make her husband a cuckold.'[1]

It was on 25 February 1661 that she gave birth to 'a strapping, blue-eyed daughter' who was baptised Anne; Roger claimed her as his child and so did the King, but she was generally thought to be the offspring of the Earl of Chesterfield whom, according to Lord Dartmouth, she much resembled. Her mother, as we have seen, considered that the King was her father but Roger was not to be denied this child. In his eyes she was his own daughter and he lavished affection on her, took her down to Dorney as a little girl and in later years made her his trustee and chief beneficiary under his will. As a joint celebration of her birth and of the Restoration he and his half-brother Philip had a new porch of brick, to match the Tudor tower, built on to Dorney Church with the date '1661' bravely inscribed above the door. Later Sir Godfrey Kneller was to paint a portrait of Anne which still hangs in the great hall of Dorney, the folds of her gown still as fresh and clear as the day he painted them, her eyes bright and compelling turned full on the beholder.

Roger had set his heart on obtaining the Marshalship of the King's Bench Prison, a lucrative office. He petitioned the King—who did not importune Charles that year after his Restoration?—writing that he had 'promoted the Royal cause at the utmost hazard of life and great loss of fortune'. Eventually, thanks to the intervention of his wife in his favour, Roger obtained the coveted office. Honours also came the way of Philip Palmer, with equal justification, for Charles knighted him for his services to the Crown and appointed him his Cupbearer.

On 20 April 1661, Pepys went to see 'The Humersome Lieutenant', as he termed it, otherwise *The Humorous Lieutenant*, by Beaumont and Fletcher, 'acted before the King, and not very well done; but my pleasure was great to see the manner of it, and so many great beauties, but above all Mrs. Palmer, with whom the King do discover a great deal of familiarity.'²

So great, in fact, that Charles decided that he must find a way of keeping her near him permanently, even after he was married. For it had now been decided that the King should marry the Infanta of Portugal, Catherine of Braganza. The only way to have Barbara close to him after his marriage would be make her a Lady of the Bedchamber, but to achieve this she must be of noble rank and to achieve that Barbara's husband must be ennobled.

On 6 October and again on 8 November the King issued an instruction for a warrant, and on 7 December Pepys wrote:

'To the Privy Seale and sealed there; and among other things that passed, there was a patent for Roger Palmer, Madame Palmer's husband, to be Earl of Castlemaine and Baron Limbricke in Ireland; but the honour is tied up to the males got of the body of this wife, the Lady Barbary; the reason whereof everybody knows.'³

This was a bitter honour for Roger; Castlemaine is a small place at the head of Dingle Bay in County Kerry at the south-western extremity of Ireland and he knew that the Earldom was simply bestowed on him to enable the King to continue his affair with his wife, from whom he was in consequence growing more and more estranged.

On 30 June 1661, Pepys wrote that

'This day, the Portuguese Embassador came to White Hall to take leave of the King; he being now going to end all with the Queen, and to send her over.'⁴

The preliminaries for this wedding went back to before the Civil War and were a reflection of that Ancient Alliance which had bound England and Portugal for nearly three centuries—since an English Princess, Philippa of Lancaster, daughter of John of Gaunt, had married João I of Portugal in 1387. The dynasty of Aviz, then founded, ruled Portugal for 200 years, petering out with the Cardinal King Henrique whose death in 1580 left the way open for Philip of Spain to seize the Portuguese throne.

Sixty disastrous years for Portugal followed. Philip used her as a springboard for attacks against English shipping and her ports for fitting out some of the ships for his Armada, with the result that in 1589, Queen Elizabeth I ordered Sir Francis Drake to destroy some of Portugal's coastal fortifications. Among them was Sagres, the navigational school of Prince Henry the Navigator, Philippa of Lancaster's illustrious son—a bitter commentary on human history.

The legitimate line of João I and Philippa had died out but there remained another, the House of Braganza, which originated with João's bastard son Affonso by Dona Inez Pires, who was his mistress before he married Philippa. In 1640 the head of this house was João, Duke of Braganza, and the hope of Portugal. He had a little daughter, who had been born on St. Catherine's Day, 1638, and on her second birthday, the Portuguese nobles sent envoys secretly to the family seat at Vila Vicosa to beg Dom João to accept the leadership of the Resistance movement and to claim the throne of Portugal. Loath to promote bloodshed, the Duke hesitated, but his Spanish wife, Dona Luzia de Medina Sidonia, picked up the two-year-old Catherine and held her up to her father, saying, 'How can you find it in your heart to refuse to make this child a King's daughter?' This tipped the scales; a week later, a pistol shot fired in Lisbon was the signal for the start of the revolt. In two days it was all over, the Spaniards had fled and Portugal was free again after sixty years; Catherine was brought to Lisbon by her father on 3 December 1640, as the Infanta of Portugal.

While the other European powers hesitated, Charles I of England was the first to recognize João IV as rightful King of Portugal. An idea began to germinate in João's mind, and in 1644 he instructed his Ambassador to approach Charles regarding a marriage between the Prince of Wales, then fourteen and the six-year-old Catherine. Charles, fearing what the English would say to another Catholic Queen, hesitated and the Civil War rendered the plan impossible, even had he wished it, so no progress was made, much to the disappointment of the Portuguese; but the plan was not completely forgotten even when the Roundheads triumphed, Charles I was beheaded and his son fled to the Low Countries while Oliver Cromwell ruled in his stead.

Catherine was educated at a nunnery in Lisbon 'just inside the great gate that leads to Alcantara'. One of its benefactresses was

Queen Henrietta Maria of England. The Infanta's education was closely supervised by her Spanish mother, Dona Luzia; from her she inherited her dark eyes and her superbly shaped hands and feet, while her easygoing father bequeathed her his good nature, which was to stand her in good stead in troublous days ahead. On his death, João bequeathed his daughter the island of Madeira and the city of Lamego in mainland Portugal.

The first Parliament held in England after Charles II's Coronation met at Westminster on 8 May 1661, and to it the King announced his intention of marrying 'the daughter of Portugal.' Addresses of congratulation to him were made in both houses five days later and on the 23rd the Portuguese Ambassador, Dom Francisco de Mello, Catherine's godfather, wrote to her brother, the new King, to announce the good news. This was followed by a Treaty of Alliance, signed in June, by which Portugal ceded Bombay to England and thus gave her her first foothold on the Indian sub-continent. This Treaty was a momentous document, as its forebear, the Treaty of Windsor of 1386, had been; great hopes were set upon it in Portugal that the first Portuguese Queen of England would be as well-loved and successful as the only English Queen of Portugal had been.

On 2 July Charles II wrote to Catherine for the first time, using the Spanish language. It was agreed that Catherine should bring in her dowry Tangier, conquered at the cost of so much Portuguese blood in years gone by, and Pepys's patron, the Earl of Sandwich, was sent to drive out the Moorish pirates who still infested it. On 10 November Pepys was at St. Gregory's Church by St. Paul's 'where I hear our Queen Katherine the first time publickly prayed for.'[5] On 28 March 1662, the Earl of Sandwich's fleet sailed into the Tagus and the Spanish vessels blockading the port scattered in confusion before it. On 1 April he was received by the Queen Mother and Catherine, handed over Charles's letters to them both and presented to the future Queen of England the English gentlemen who were appointed to her household.

Three weeks later Catherine and her suite embarked at Lisbon in the *Royal Charles,* the Princess bidding her mother and brother and homeland a tearful farewell. The voyage was delayed by north-west winds; Pepys went down to Portsmouth in vain and returned to London. On 7 May he wrote,

'Mr. Montagu is last night come to the King with news, that he left the Queen and flete in the Bay of Biscay, coming this wayward; and he believes she is now at the Isle of Scilly.'[6]

The following day he wrote that Sir George Carteret had told him that the Queen and fleet were in Mount's Bay 'on Monday last.' This delighted the Cornishmen who, while their new Queen's ship sheltered in the lee of the land, sent up fireworks and salvoes to welcome her.

On the 14th Catherine arrived at Portsmouth; the Duke of York had gone out with five ships to meet Sandwich's fleet and was received very sweetly by his future sister-in-law; he remarked on her gentleness, humility and dignity. She was received on shore by the Dukes of Manchester and Ormonde and by her godfather, the Portuguese Ambassador, and was then conducted to her lodgings in the *Domus Dei,* where her principal Lady of the Bedchamber, Barbara's aunt, the Countess of Suffolk, received her. On the 17th Pepys went down to Hampton Court and saw all made ready for her; the same day the King besought Parliament that 'steps should be taken at once to make her first view of London should not be unflattering' and a major cleaning operation ensued. Three days later, after a night ride, he met his bride for the first time, 'Catherine keeping her bedde by reason of a sore throat'. The following day a secret Catholic wedding ceremony was performed in her bedchamber by Lord Aubigny, a secular priest, to be followed in public in the Presence Chamber by a Church of England marriage performed by the Bishop of London. Two days later, Charles wrote to his sister Henrietta, 'Madame', Duchess of Orleans, to say he was delighted with his bride and next day a kindly letter of welcome for Catherine arrived from the Queen Mother, Henrietta Maria.

Meanwhile Barbara Palmer had been keeping to her lodging.

'We went to the theatre to see "The French Dancing Mistress" '
wrote Pepys

'and there with much pleasure saw and gazed upon Lady Castlemaine; but it troubles me to see hei look dejectedly and slighted by people already.'[7]

Sarah, Lord Sandwich's housekeeper, who was a mine of useful information for Pepys, told him that, prior to the news of the arrival of Catherine's ship in Mount's Bay,

'the King had dined at my Lady Castlemaine's and supped
every day and night the last week'
but that on the night of 13 May, when
'the bonfires were made for joy of the Queen's arrival, the King
was there; but there was no fire at her door, although all the rest
of the doors almost in the street; which was much observed;
and that she and the King did send for a pair of scales and
weighed one another and she, being with child, was said to be
the heaviest.'
But on the 19th he wrote,
'she is now a most disconsolate creature and comes not out of
the doors since the King's going.'
On 21 May, the day of the royal wedding at Portsmouth, Pepys
and his wife went to Lord Sandwich's lodging at Whitehall, next
door to Barbara's lodging, 'my Lord being with the King and Queen'
and there, looking into next door from the privy-garden where he
walked, saw
'the finest smocks and linnen petticoats of my Lady
Castlemaine's laced with rich lace at the bottom, that mine eyes
ever beheld; it did me good to look at them.'⁹
On the 31st he wrote
'The Queen is brought a few days since to Hampton Court; and
all people say of her to be a very fine and handsome lady, and
very discreet; and that the King is pleased enough with her;
which, I fear, will put Madame Castlemaine's nose out of
joynt.'¹⁰
The young Portuguese Queen was aware of 'the Lady's'
influence and was determined that she should not come near her.
The King was equally determined that she should. This problem
was therefore added to Catherine's natural difficulties in adjusting
herself to the manners and customs of a strange country.
Unfortunately the strict etiquette and even the dress of the
Portuguese court did nothing to help Catherine and they became
the object of ribald mirth in Charles's court. Portugal's sixty-year
subjugation by Spain had left its mark and the ladies were wearing
clothes which went out of fashion in England at the end of the
reign of Elizabeth. Pepys went to Charing Cross with his friend
Captain Ferrers
'and there at the Triumph taverne he showed me some

Portugall ladyes, which are come to Towne before the Queen. They are not handsome and their farthingales a strange dress. Many ladies and persons of quality come to see them; I find nothing in them that is pleasing and I see they have learnt to kiss and look freely up and down already and I do believe will soon forget the recluse practice of their own country.'[11]

The diarists admired Catherine herself, whatever they felt about her suite. Evelyn, more sober in his style than Pepys, wrote:

'The Queene arrived with a traine of Portuguese ladies in their monstrous fardingales or guard-infantas, their complexions olivader and sufficiently unagreeable. Her Majesty in the same habit, her foretop long and turn'd aside very strangely. She was yet of the handsomest countenance of all the rest and tho' low of stature prettily shaped, languishing and excellent eyes, her teeth wronging her mouth by sticking a little too far out; for the rest lovely enough.'

As for the King, he was delighted with his bride; on 23 May 1662 he wrote to his sister Madame:

'My Lord St. Albans will give you so full a description of my wife as I shall not go about to do it, only I must tell you I think myself very happy. I was married the day before yesterday, but the fortune that follows our family is fallen upon me, *car Monsieur le Cardinal m'a fermé la porte au nez* and though I am not so furious as Monsieur was, but am content to let those pass over before I go to bed with my wife, yet I hope I shall entertain her better the first night than he did you.'[12]

To his mother-in-law, Queen Luzia of Portugal, he wrote:

'Being now freed from dread of the sea and enjoying in this springtime the company of my dearest wife, I am the happiest man in the world and the most enamoured, seeing at close hand the loveliness of her person and her virtues . . . I wish to say of my wife that I cannot sufficiently either look at her or talk to her.'

From Portsmouth, on 21 May, he had written amusingly enough to Clarendon:

'I arrived here yesterday about two in the afternoon and as soon as I had shifted myself I went to my wife's chamber, where I found her in bed, by reason of a little cough, and some inclination to a fever, which was caused, as we physicians say,

by having certain things stopped at sea which ought to have
carried away those humours. But now all is in their due course,
and I believe she will find herself very well in the morning as
soon as she wakes.

'It was happy for the honour of the nation that I was not put
to the consummation of the marriage last night; for I was so
sleepy by having slept but two hours in my journey as I was
afraid that matters would have gone very sleepily. I can now
only give you an account of what I have seen a-bed; which, in
short is, that her face is not so exact as to be called a beauty,
though her eyes are excellent good, and not anything in her
face that in the least degree can shock one. On the contrary, she
has as much agreeableness in her looks as ever I saw; and if I
have any skill in phyisiognomy, which I think I have, she must
be as good a woman as ever was born. Her conversation, as
much as I can perceive, is very good; for she has wit enough and
a most agreeable voice. You would much wonder to see how
well we are acquainted already. In a word, I think myself very
happy.'¹ ³

So all seemed set fair, when the royal couple made their way
from Portsmouth to Hampton Court, but the adroit and seductive
Barbara did not have long in fact to sulk, for less than a fortnight
later, on 6 June, Pepys wrote that he went to supper with My
Lady Sandwich,

'who tells me, with much trouble, that my Lady Castlemaine is
still as great with the King and the King comes to her as often as
he ever did.'¹ ⁴

A few days later Charles, Barbara's second child, was born at her
house at King Street. Roger, who had by then finally embraced
the Catholic faith, gave orders that he should be baptised by a
Roman priest. Barbara was still a Protestant, and a violent quarrel
ensued between them. On 18 June Barbara contrived to have her
baby—who was doubtless the King's child—baptised yet again, this
time by the Rector of St. Margaret's, Westminster, who noted in
his Register, 'Charles Palmer, Ld. Limbricke,s. to ye right honble
Roger, Earl of Castlemaine, by Barbara.' The godparents were the
King, the Earl of Oxford and Barbara's aunt, the Countess of
Suffolk, as Pepys was duly informed by the obliging Sarah.

'Prior to this, on the 16th,'

he wrote

> 'I was told that my Lady Castlemaine having quite fallen out
> from her husband, did yesterday go away from him, taking
> with her all her plate, jewels and other best things, every dish
> and cloth and servant, except the porter and is gone to
> Richmond to a brother of hers which, I am apt to think, was a
> design to get out of town, that the King might come to her the
> better.'

No doubt the perspicacious Samuel was quite right. Barbara had
been waiting for the excuse of a quarrel over the baptism to leave
Roger, who bored her. Sarah told Pepys the reason things had
come to this pass— 'how the falling out between my Lady
Castlemaine and her Lord was about the christening of the child
lately.' It was not a brother in fact to whom she betook herself at
Richmond, but an uncle, Colonel Edward Villiers, a Groom of the
Bedchamber to James, Duke of York, and she had been at his
house less than three months when she contrived to get accepted
at Hampton Court and on 16 July was permitted to kiss the
Queen's hand.

Lord Chancellor Clarendon, aware of the King's intentions,
encouraged Catherine of Braganza to resist the plan to make
Barbara a Lady of the Bedchamber and for his pains received a
very pointed letter from Charles:

> 'I forgot when you were last here to desire you to give
> Broderick good counsel, not to meddle any more with what
> concerns Lady Castlemaine, and to let him have a care how he is
> the author of any scandalous reports. For if I find him guilty of
> any such thing, I will make him repent it to the last moment of
> his life. And now I am entered on this matter, I think it
> necessary to give you a little good counsel in it, lest you may
> think that, by making a further stir in the business, you may
> divert me from my resolution, which all the world shall never
> do. And I wish I may be unhappy in this world and the world to
> come if I fail in the least degree of what I have resolved, which is
> of making my Lady Castlemaine of my wife's bedchamber.
> And whosoever I find use any endeavour to hinder this
> resolution of mine (except it be only myself) I will be his
> enemy to the last moment of my life.'[16]

Poor Catherine! Though she made a scene with the King and did her utmost to prevent it, on 23 August Barbara became a Lady of the Queen's Bedchamber and, when the Court moved back to Whitehall, was assigned lodgings in a part of the Palace separated from the main buildings. Pepys foresaw it all:

> 'I hear the Queen did prick her out of the list presented her by the King; desiring that she might have that favour done her, or that he would send her from whence she came; and that the King was angry and the Queen discontented a whole day and night upon it; but that the King hath promised to have nothing to do with her hereafter. But I cannot believe that the King can fling her off so, he loving her too well.'[17]

Such indeed was the case, as Catherine's private physician observed, and Pepys noted

> 'that the Queen do know how the King orders things, and how he carried himself to my Lady Castlemaine and others, as well as any body; but though she hath spirit enough, yet seeing that she do no good by taking notice of it, for the present she forebears it in policy; of which I am very glad.'[18]

Pepys noted admiringly that Barbara, in addition to being beautiful, could have a care for the under-dog in an age which cared little for those of lowly birth. When Charles brought Catherine by barge to Whitehall from Hampton Court a great stand had been erected on the bank for the public to witness the ceremony; under the weight of humanity the scaffolding collapsed on 'the rabble' and alone of all the ladies, her hair flying in the wind, Barbara rushed down to succour an injured child. Then Pepys noted that 'there came one booted and spurred and being in her hair' Barbara borrowed his plumed Cavalier's hat to protect her coiffure. Swift and decisive in emergency, gay and informal in the oddest circumstance, it was small wonder that Barbara, the most sparkling and unusual of all the Court ladies, endeared herself so deeply to the King.

Her triumph was complete and Roger left alone and disconsolate. Foreseeing where her extravagance could lead him, he obtained a bond engaging the Earl of Sandwich and Viscount Grandison

> 'in the summe of ten thousand pounds to indemnify him from all and every manner of debts, contracts and sums of money now due, or that hereafter shall grow due, from any contract or

bargain made by ye Right Honble Barbara, Countess of Castlemaine.'[19]
without his express consent or direction.

So 'the Lady' remained ever before the Queen, who 'takes all with the greatest meekness that may be.' On New Year's Day, 1663, Pepys was told by Mrs. Sarah that

'the King sups at least four times every week with her, and goes through the garden alone privately, and that so that the very sentrys take notice of it and speak of it; and that about a month ago Lady Castlemaine quickened at My Lord Gerard's at dinner, and cried out that she was undone; and all the lords and men were fain to quit the room, and women called to help her.'[20]

On 3rd of the same month Pepys, walking in Whitehall, 'did see the King coming privately from my Lady Castlemaine's, which is a poor thing for a Prince to do'[21] but Pepys being Pepys failed to appreciate that as Barbara had just suffered a miscarriage this visit could only be attributed to the King's great considerateness. Pepys remained bewitched by her beauty. On 1 March 1663 (Lord's Day) he wrote:

'After sermon a very fine anthem; so I up into the house among the courtiers, seeing the fine ladies and above all my Lady Castlemaine, who is above all, that only she I can observe for true beauty.'[22]

By the summer, however, he had noted a drastic change, albeit she was not yet twenty-three:

'I saw my Lady Castlemaine, who, I fear, is not so handsome as I have taken her for, and now she begins to decay something. This is my wife's opinion also, for which I am sorry.'[23]

Her appointment as Lady of the Bedchamber to the reluctant Queen had now been confirmed by Royal Warrant. Her aunt, the Countess of Suffolk, was already First Lady of the Bedchamber and Mistress of the Robes. Barbara now had full opportunity to visit Catherine and insult her. Pepys related

'of a wipe the Queene a little while ago did give her, when she came in and found the Queene under the dresser's hands and had been so long. "I wonder your Majesty" says she "can have the patience to sit so long a-dressing?" "I have so much reason, to use patience" says the Queene "that I can very well bear with it." '2 4

Barbara was then seven months with a child who came into the world on 28 September and was baptised Henry. He was doubtless the King's child, though of all Barbara's offspring he was the one whom Charles delayed longest in recognizing, but by the end of the year his mother was pregnant again by her royal lover.

VI

PINEAPPLE ROYAL
(1663–1669)

AFTER THEIR separation, Roger could bear Barbara's proximity no longer. Pepys relates how, on 14 September 1662, he was in a garden near Whitehall and there observed Roger and Barbara walking up and down. The first time they passed, Roger lifted his hat and bowed to his wife and she dropped him a curtsey, but thereafter they passed each other without speaking or indicating that they were aware of each other's presence; only, when they came abreast of the baby, Charles, whom the nurse was carrying, they would each in turn pause, take him from the nurse's arms and dandle him, handing him back before the other spouse arrived again.[1]

In 1663 Roger left England for the Continent and travelled extensively in France and Italy; 1664 saw him serving in the Venetian naval squadron commanded by the celebrated Admiral Andrea Cornaro, which went to the relief of Candia in Crete, then besieged by the Turks. Roger's seafaring experience over the next few years was destined to be quite considerable. In fact he returned in 1665 to northern waters and for two years saw service in the English fleet commanded by James, Duke of York, in the war against the Dutch, whom it defeated off Lowestoft on 1 June 1665.

On 22 December 1663, the French Ambassador wrote to Louis XIV that Lady Castlemaine had been converted to the Catholic faith

'and the King of England, when the Lady's parents begged him to put some obstacle in her way, replied gallantly that he did

36

not meddle with ladies' souls.'

Pepys remarked that the Queen did not like it much, 'thinking that she do it not for conscience sake.' On 20 January, 1664, Pepys wrote

'that the King do not openly disavow my Lady Castlemaine, but that she comes to Court; but that my Lord Fitzharding, and the Hamiltons, and sometime my Lord Sandwich, they say, intrigue with her. But he says my Lord Sandwich will lead her from her lodgings in the darkest and obscurest manner, and leave her at the entrance to the Queene's. lodgings, that he might be the least observed.'

On 1 February the King was at the theatre and Barbara in the next box; she leant over some other ladies to whisper to him and then went into the King's box and sat down between him and the Duke of York

'which he swares put the King himself, as well as everybody else, out of countenance; and believes that she only did it to show the world that she is not out of favour yet, as was believed.'

On 18 April Pepys observed in Hyde Park 'my Lady Castlemaine in a coach by herself, in yellow satin with a pinner on.' Barbara affected yellows and browns, which suited her colouring, and is dressed in amber in the famous Lely painting now at Dorney Court which Pepys so much wanted to see and failed to do so when he called at the artist's studio. He did, however, much admire another Lely painting of her which Lady Sandwich showed to him and his wife on July 10.

Meanwhile Barbara had been providing the Court gossips with their usual quota of scandal and excitement. On 25 January 1664, there was a fire in her lodgings, the cause of which was unknown and on the 27th special orders were issued for fire-fighting equipment to be installed. On 5 September Barbara gave birth to a daughter, who was christened Charlotte and was almost certainly the offspring of the King. A fortnight later she was destined to undergo an unpleasant experience when returning home through St. James's Park from a visit to the Duchess of York at St. James's Palace. Barbara was accompanied only by a little page and a maid, when three masked men suddenly leapt out in front of her, upbraided her and insulted her, telling her that Edward IV's mistress, Jane Shore, had died on a dunghill despised and forsaken by all and that a similar fate would shortly befall her.

On reaching Whitehall, Barbara collapsed. A message was sent to the King, who had the Park gates closed and everybody inside arrested, but the masked men had disappeared and the seven or eight people found within were all innocent and had to be released.

On March 19 Pepys observed the first day of the coach outings in Hyde Park 'where many brave ladies', among others, 'Castlemaine lay impudently upon her back in her coach asleep with her mouth open'. The rivalry between her and Frances Stewart had then reached its height, with the King paying both visits. Barbara left Whitehall with the rest of the Court on 29 June 1665, to escape the Great Plague which Pepys had first noticed three weeks before; it had now got a firm hold on the unhappy inhabitants of London and it was deemed imprudent for the King and his courtiers to remain at Whitehall, so they exchanged that Palace for Hampton Court.

We now come to the story of the pineapple, a persistent tradition in Dorney up to this day and one handed down in the Palmer family for 300 years. This says that some time that summer, or very soon after, the King was brought a present from Sir Philip and Lady Palmer at Dorney Court; this was the first pineapple grown in England which Rose, Sir Philip's gardener, had produced at Dorney. Evelyn records that he

'first saw the famous *Queen Pine* brought from Barbados and presented to his Majesty; but the first that were seen in England were those sent to Cromwell four years since.'[2]

Evelyn wrote this on 9 August 1661; evidently the present then was an importation but now native-grown pineapples were shown to be possible. The taste became established and Evelyn himself records eating one at a banquet three years later.[3]

On 27 July the Court, fearing the spread of the Plague, left Hampton and proceeded west to Salisbury, where they spent the rest of the summer; then on 25 September they moved on to Oxford, where the King took up residence in Christ Church. Queen Catherine arrived the following day and entered her quarters at Merton where they remained over Christmas. On 28 December Barbara caused a stir by giving birth to a son in the chamber of one of the Fellows of the College.

On New Year's Day, 1666, the baby was baptised with the name of George. Some four years afterwards a chaplain entered the following in the fly-leaf of the Register for Merton College Chapel:

> '28th December 1665. Georg Palmer base sone of King Charles ye 2 was born in Merton Coll. Bapt. there ye first of Jan. His mother's name was Barbara, daughter of Villiers, wife of Roger E. of Castlemaine and now she is Duchess of Cleveland.'

Barbara carried if off with her usual aplomb but the little Queen, who so much wanted to bear Charles an heir, was less fortunate; Merton was to be for her a place of sad memories, for she suffered a miscarriage almost simultaneously with Barbara's successful delivery.

Roger, meanwhile, had been occupying himself in a different manner. In July the Fleet put to sea again with the intention of intercepting De Ruyter's Altantic squadron and the richly-laden Dutch East Indiamen, but the latter eluded them. However, at the end of August the Dutch put to sea again, and on 4 September Roger took part in the Battle of Solebay, in which the British fleet was victorious and captured at least twelve prizes, including four first class ships of the line. In the course of this action the Earl of Sandwich was killed.

Two days earlier on 2 September 1666, an event occurred of even wider importance to a greater number of people. In a baker's shop in the City began the Great Fire, which sped at great speed through the timber buildings and tortuous alleys of London. The hapless refugees watched in horror from the south bank the destruction of their city, including the great mediaeval Cathedral of St. Paul.

The King was in the forefront of the battle, encouraging the fire-fighters and the homeless and immediately after it died down set about planning the reconstruction, giving great scope to his brilliant architect, Sir Christopher Wren. Though much of beauty and priceless value was destroyed, it could at least be said that all traces of the Plague of the year before were eradicated and spaciousness and grace replaced a haphazard jumble of buildings.

Roger carefully noted down details of his naval actions and of his travels. In 1666 he wrote *An Account of the Present War between the Venetians and the Turks with the state of Candia* in a letter to the King which he wrote from Venice. He also prepared an account of the Dutch naval war which, able linguist that he was, he wrote in French; it was eventually translated into English in 1671 by Thomas Price under the title *A short and true Account of the Material Passages in the late War between the English and the Dutch*. About the same time Roger published *The Catholique Apology*, a vindication of the loyalty of English Roman Catholics, which, considering the danger to which it exposed him, was a courageous act. It was a lucid, eloquent document. Pepys read it on 1 December, without knowing the identity of the author and declared it to be 'very well writ indeed.' Roger's theory was that there was no reason, just because they chose to follow the Catholic faith, why his co-religionists in England should be any less loyal to the Crown than their Protestant fellows. He had indeed a good precedent on which to draw, for at the time of greatest danger from a Papist invasion, in 1588, Queen Elizabeth, that unswervingly Protestant monarch, had placed in command in her fleet to defend the country against the Armada a Papist, Lord Howard of Effingham, who had brilliantly fulfilled her trust. Unhappily these were not the days of Good Queen Bess; eleven years of Puritanism had left their indelible mark and Roger's enemies remembered *The Catholique Apology* and bided their time.

Roger was well rid of Barbara. It was said that by December 1666, the King had paid no less than £30,000 to clear off her debts. Early the following year she had an intrigue with Henry Jermyn later Earl of St. Albans; her days as the King's mistress were becoming interspersed with favours shown to others and in the summer of 1667 she bore Charles his last child by her, which died in infancy. Nevertheless her influence on the King continued unabated and she obtained favour for friends and relatives and disgrace for her enemies. On 17 July she procured the release of her cousin, the Duke of Buckingham, from the Tower of London and on 26 August achieved her master-stroke, the disgrace of the Lord Chancellor Clarendon, who was forced to resign his Seals of Office largely at her instigation.

Clarendon, extremely competent but generally unloved, had been the King's chief minister since the Restoration. Charles chafed at what he regarded as the paternalistic tutelage of Clarendon; the minister had also upset many factions, not least the moderates when he obstructed the King's desire to achieve greater religious tolerance by repealing the Act of Uniformity. Clarendon's daughter, Anne Hyde, had been the mistress and later became the wife of James, Duke of York, whose conversion to Catholicism did not endear him to the mass of his brother's subjects. The *coup de grâce* to Clarendon's unpopularity was however given when the Dutch fleet, under De Ruyter and Cornelis de Wit, sailed up the Medway in the summer of 1667, ran the gauntlet of the guns of Upnor Castle—hastily strengthened by Monk—smashed through the boom he had thrown across the river and sent fireships in amongst the first-rate ships in dock, ending by towing the flagship ignominiously out to sea.

The policy which had brought the United Provinces into war with England and in particular the policy which had laid up the Fleet were laid at Clarendon's door. Egged on by her friend Baron Arlington, the former Sir Henry Bennet, who loathed Clarendon, Barbara prevailed upon the King to dismiss the Chancellor. Accusations of high treason against him failed to get through the Lords, however, though both Houses passed an Act of Parliament, as a result of which the unhappy Clarendon died in exile in Rouen.

Peace between England and the United Provinces and their ally France was signed at Breda in June 1667, and Roger Palmer thus found himself free of his naval service, to return home, as the French Ambassador Commings sarcastically wrote to his master, Louis XIV, to discover that 'two of his children had been born in his absence.' Roger was now a man of considerable substance, fortunately for his half-brother Sir Philip and for Dorney. That same year Philip had gone surety for the payment of £11,000 due from Dudley Rouse, the Receiver General of Land Tax for Oxfordshire, and when he failed, Sir Philip, unable to meet the liability, was threatened with confiscation of his estates; in order to preserve them he conveyed them to his half-brother Roger, who therefore, for the time being at least, became the titular Lord of Dorney. He did not stay in England, however, to enjoy the estate but early in 1668 accompanied Sir Daniel Harvey on his mission to the Porte, where the latter was appointed British Ambassador to the Court of the Great Sultan.

While Roger was in Constantinople he was evidently held in very high esteem by the Turks. His friendly reception (for he had fought against them at Candia) may well have been due in part to the presence in Constantinople of a cousin, Thomas, nicknamed 'Whiskers' Palmer, some eighteen months younger than Roger, who had for some years been a leading merchant of the Levant and Near East, and who was a younger son of Sir Thomas, the second Wingham baronet. The whiskers he wore according to the custom of Turkey and even in the latter part of his life, when he returned to London, he did not cut them off and so received the nickname. He married Lucy, daughter of Thomas Young, merchant of London, descended from an ancient Devon family of Axminster. He died very rich and left most of his fortune to his nephew Sir Thomas, the fourth Wingham baronet. On his return to Dorney he brought with him the portaits of seven eminent Turks, which hang in the great hall of Dorney Court to this day, with a plaque reading 'Seven eminent Turks circa 1668. Presented to Lord Castlemaine during his Embassy to Constantinople.' As the Turks were not prone to allow their portaits to be painted for anyone, least of all for an infidel, this speaks highly enough of the regard in which they held him.

Charles and Barbara's passion for each other had now cooled, though 'the Lady' retained great influence over the King. On 4 April 1668, Pepys noted that she was having an affair with Charles Hart, great-nephew of Shakespeare and a famous tragic actor. Somewhere about the same time the King made Moll Davis of the Duke's Theatre—'the most impertinent slut in the world'—his mistress. Nevertheless, Barbara remained in high favour at Court. Evelyn wrote that he

> 'saw the tragedy of "Horace" acted before their Majesties. 'Twixt each act a masq and antiq daunce. The excessive jewellery of the ladies was infinite, those especially on that . . . . . . Castlemaine esteem'd at £40,000 and more, far outshining the Queene.'[6]

The same year a curious event took place. On 24 March 1668, the London apprentices, fired apprently by religious zeal, started pulling down the brothels in the city. The very next day *The Poor Whores Petition* was published and sent to Barbara Palmer. As an impudent document it was without peer. Headed 'The Humble

Petition of the Undone Company of poore distressed Whores, Bawds, Pimps and Panders', it began:

'That Your Petitioners having been for a long time connived at and countenanced in the practice of our Venereal pleasures (a Trade wherein your Ladyship hath great experience and for your diligence therein, have arrived at high and Eminent Advancement for these late years . . . '

The writers implored

'Your Honour to improve your Interest which (all know) is great, that some speedy Relief may be afforded us to prevent our Utter Ruine and Undoing.'[7]

It was signed by 'Madam Cresswell' and 'Damaris Page', the latter, Pepys states, being 'the great bawd of seamen.'

'The Gracious Answer' was published on 24 April—*Dio Veneris 24 April*—and was a lengthy document. It was addressed to

'Right Trusty and Well-Beloved Madam Cresswell and Damaris Page and the rest of the suffering Sisterhood in Dog and Bitch Yard, Lakeners Lane, Saffron-Hill, Moor-fields, Rattcliffe-Highway, etc. We greet you well, in giving you to understand our Noble Mind by returning our Thanks, which you are worthy of, in rendering us our Titles of Honour, which are but our Due . . . '

It continued

'Splendidly did we appear upon the Theatre at W.H. being to amazement wonderfully decked with Jewels and Diamonds, which the (abhorred and to be undone) Subjects of this Kingdom have payed for. We have been also Serene and Illustrious ever since the Day that *Mars* was so instrumental to restore our Godess *Venus* to her Temple and Worship; where, by special Grant we quickly became a Famous Lady; And as a Reward of our Devotion, soon created Right Honourable, the Countess of *Castlemain*.'

There followed a tirade against the Church of England:

'according to the ancient Rules and laudable Customs of our Order, we have *cum privilegio* alwayes (without our Husband) satisfied our self with the Delights of *Venus:* and in our Husbands absence have had a numerous off-spring (which are bountifully and Nobly provided for). Which Practice hath Episcopal Allowance also, according to the principles of Seer

Shelden, etc. *If women have not children by their own
Husbands, they are bound (to prevent their Damnation) to try
by using the means with other Men;* which wholesome and
pleasing Doctrine did for some time hold me fast to his Religion.
But since this Seer hath shown more Cowardize, than Principles
or Policy, in fearing to declare the Church of *Rome* to be the
True, Ancient, Uniform, Universal and most Holy Mother
Church; Therefore we tell you (with all the Sisterhood) That
we are now no longer of the Church of *England,* which is but
like a Brazen Bason tied to a Barbers wooden Pole, (viz)
Protestant Doctrine and Order tied by Parliamentary Power to
Roman Catholick Foundations, Constitutions, and Rights, etc.'
etc.'

A long list of *Items,* each quite outrageous, then followed, the last
reading

'To any other than here directed, give no Entertainment
without Ready Money, lest you suffer Loss. For had we not
been careful in that particular, we had neither gained Honour
nor Rewards, which are now (as you know) both conferred
upon us.   CASTLEM.....

'Given at our Closset in
King street Westminster,
Die Veneris April 24, 1668.'

Both the great diarists observed the publication of these
documents. Evelyn remarked,

'Amongst other libertine libels there was one now printed, and
thrown about, a bold petition of the poor whores to Lady
Castlemaine'

and Pepys wrote that

'my Lady Castlemaine is horribly vexed at the late libell, the
petition of the poor prostitutes about the town, whose houses
were pulled down the other day. I have got one of them, and it
is not very witty, but devilish severe against her and the King;
and I wonder how it durst be printed and spread abroad, which
shews that times are loose, and come to a great disregard of the
King, or Court, or Government.'

It was indeed to be Barbara's fate throughout most of her life to
be the object of scurrilous verses, pamphlets and lampoons; but, as
her biographer wrote, by satisfying the pleasures of a Prince she

excited much envy.[8]

The same month the King made Barbara a present of Berkshire House. This was the residence of the Earls of Berkshire in the Parish of St. Martin-in-the-Fields and stood entirely alone at the corner of St. James's Street opposite St. James's Palace. It had a large walled garden with a summer house, an ideal place for bringing up children, and thither Barbara at once removed with her offspring. She looked after the King's children well enough and Charles, though he was now, as Saint-Simon declares in his *Memoirs,* 'nothing more than a good friend', took an interest in the furnishing of Berkshire House and visited Barbara to see how it was progressing. But Pepys wrote on May 31 that 'Lady Castlemaine is, it seems, mightily melancholy and discontented.' Later the same year, on 21 December 1668, Pepys saw the King and Moll Davis exchanging amorous glances at the Theatre and observed that 'my Lady Castlemaine, on perceiving who it was that attracted the King's notice, looked like fire.' Barbara had meanwhile despatched her eldest daughter, Anne, now aged seven, to be educated at a French monastery at Chaillot near Paris, which had been founded by Queen Henrietta Maria for the nuns of the Visitation of St. Mary and thereby began a long and at times eventful connection of Anne with France. She was brought back to England the first time in 1669.

During Roger's absence abroad his sister-in-law, Lady Phoebe Palmer, had died at the age of forty-eight on 12 August 1668 and was buried in the vault at Dorney. On 22 September Roger wrote to Philip from Vienna. He commiserated with him on his wife's death and advised him not to marry again; he continued with other practical advice:

'In the first place I would not have you keep house because you will spend more in it on unnecessary servants and hangers-on than you would do at Court or anywhere else, for the Court itself is no expense to a prudent single man. All that you need is to have a care that the house be in repair and come among the tenants at necessary times. In the next place, for your eldest son, if you can but settle about £140 p.a. certainly paid I would advise you where there is a cheap and good Academy where for a year or two he may pass his time in learning to his great advantage and accomplishment. Thirdly for your younger sons

I would advise you to send them to their brother Harry at St. Omers for there they will fare very well and it will cost you but £50 per an. which is cheaper than you can keep them anywhere in England. Lastly for your daughter, if you send her (where Kate Darrell is) to my Lady Nevill, 'twill cost you but £30 p.an. and there she may stay until she is fit for marriage, receiving in the meantime a virtuous and good education and thus you know people of the best fashion beyond sea breed their children. This £80 per ann. for your three youngest children you must pay.

I am now going from hence to Italy because I cannot here find a safe passage to Constantinople and if I do not find some Man of War at Venice or Ligorn I do intend to stay this winter in Rome.'[9]

The considerateness of Roger is shown by this letter to his half-brother, suddenly bereft of his wife, left to cope in straitened circumstances with five children, the eldest of whom was now twenty-four and the youngest eleven. The daughter whom Roger referred to was Phoebe, eldest daughter and youngest child of Sir Philip, born in 1657.

The Lady Nevill was the English Abbess of the nunnery at Pontoise in Normandy. Sir Philip sent Phoebe, not to Pontoise, but to the Blue Nuns, in 1671 for he did not always follow Roger's advice in every particular—for example as regards remaining a widower. On 15 November 1669, he married at Gray's Inn Chapel Anne, now aged forty, widow of Sir Henry Palmer of Howletts, Kent, at whose death in 1659 she had been married to him for nineteen years and had borne him twelve children; the younger of these were now added to the responsibilities occasioned by five of Philip's own.

Meanwhile, on 16 January 1669, Pepys had been told that

'My Lady Castlemaine is now in a higher command over the King than ever—not as a mistress, for she scorns him, but as a tyrant, to command him, and . . . the Duke and Duchess of York are mighty great with her.'

This was natural, seeing that her house lay so close to St. James's Palace. Three days later Barbara received a grant, in the names of George, Viscount Grandison, and Edward Villiers, Esq., of £4,700 per annum out of the revenues of the Post Office. Edward Villiers was that same uncle to whom Barbara had betaken herself when first estranged from Roger; on April 4 Pepys found him, together with an august company which included the Duke and Duchess of York, at a dinner at the house of the Treasurer of the Navy at Deptford, where, after dinner, they played ' "I love my love with an A." . . . and some of them, but particularly the Duchess herself and my Lady Castlemaine, were very witty.'3

Her successes with the King that year included obtaining the dismissal of the Duke of Ormonde from his post as Lord Lieutentant of Ireland. The cause of her displeasure was that she had obtained a royal warrant for the grant of Phoenix Park, Dublin, but Ormonde, in his capacity of Lord Lieutenant, refused to pass it and indeed prevailed upon the King to fit the house up for himself and his successors. When he returned to England Barbara, it is reported, fell upon him with a torrent of abuse, but the Duke coolly riposted by saying he did not wish her death, only to see her old.

VII

THE MISTRESS OF CHURCHILL
(-1 6 6 9–1 6 7 3)

ROGER'S *Catholique Apology* had been answered by the Reverend William Lloyd, and Castlemaine, not unnaturally, decided to riposte. Assisted by Robert Pugh, a secular priest, he issued *A Reply to the Answer of the Catholic Apology, A Clear Vindication of the Catholics of England.* It much fitted the King's present mood, for secret negotiations were now in progress between the French and English Kings with a view to getting Charles to declare his conversion to Catholicism—in the hopes that this would bring England into France's embrace. This would have suited Louis XIV's book very well indeed and to persuade Charles to take this momentous step he employed the one person who could profoundly influence him.

This was his sister Henrietta, otherwise 'Minette', otherwise La Duchesse d'Orléans, otherwise Madame, the darling of the French Court, with whom Charles maintained an affectionate and almost daily correspondence after his restoration.

When the Parliamentary forces under the Earl of Essex had approached Exeter in August 1644 and Queen Henrietta Maria had escaped via Falmouth to France, the baby Princess remained behind, cared for by Lady Dalkeith, until the 'ever faithful' city surrendered in 1646 after a protracted siege and she was taken away to Oatlands Park in Surrey. Three months later, in July 1646, when she was just two years old, Henrietta was taken across the Channel to join her mother in France and did not see England again till 1660.

Thus Henrietta, entirely under her mother's influence, alone of all Charles I's children was brought up in the Catholic faith. When her brother Charles, after his dramatic escape from England in 1651, came to Paris, the little girl's admiration for this tall, spare, handsome brother who had suffered such great privations was enormous. They were able to be together for some years and from that time dated the great affection in which they held each other. Henrietta and her mother paid a brief visit to England in the autumn and winter of 1660/1; Pepys remarked that the Queen was by then 'a little, plain old woman', that the Princess was very pretty but he did not like the way her hair was 'frized up round the ears'. Their return to France was delayed by Henrietta developing measles on board the ship outward bound from Portsmouth: it put back and to make matters worse ran aground in the process. Eventually she recovered and returned to France with her mother in January 1661: later the same year she was married to 'Monsieur', otherwise Philipe d'Orléans, brother of Louis XIV.

When the opportunity appeared to present itself to entice England back into the fold, Louis arranged for it to take place under the cloak of a visit by Madame to her brother the King. The King and Queen of France accompanied Henrietta and her party as far as St. Omer; something went wrong with the arrangements and there was no accommodation for the Court, at which Louis grumbled excessively, but Madame made light of it, sleeping in a barn with her ladies and extracting the maximum pleasure from the situation.

She duly crossed to Dover, which Charles had done his utmost to render pleasant and galvanize into activity, in honour of his sister. Henrietta was delighted to see Charles and her native land again. Her ungracious and jealous husband had stipulated a mere week's absence, eventually extended to a fortnight by Louis XIV. Throughout that time she enjoyed herself, feted by her brother and his people, her face shining with pleasure. The Secret Treaty of Dover was in fact signed on 22 May 1670 so that 'Minette' had evidently overcome what inhibitions her brother might have had about her project. He was to announce his conversion to Catholicism 'when the affairs of his Kingdom permitted', but he contrived to insert a clause for pecuniary assistance which took Louis XIV aback. On 2 June 1670 Minette, well-pleased, returned

to France in triumph, followed out to sea by Charles and James
several miles off Dover, unable to bear parting from this dear and
beautiful sister; but though her journey had been apparently a
political and religious success, for her disaster was waiting. She
died within a few weeks of setting foot on French soil and was
mourned by the French Court and the entire nation, not to
mention her brothers and the English Court. On her departure she
had made Charles promise to look after her servants should
anything happen to her and the adroit Louis saw in this another
opportunity not to be missed, which he was to take in due course.

Charles's passions had been directed for some time towards the
beautiful Frances Stewart, but on her betrothal to the Duke of
Richmond she firmly repelled the King's advances and on
becoming Duchess left Court. Louis saw his opportunity and sent
to England one of the loveliest of Henrietta's ladies, the dark,
curvaceous Bretonne, Mademoiselle de Keroualle, ostensibly to
fulfil Madame's wish that her brother should look after one of her
closest companions, but actually to ensnare the King. So it fell
out, but not entirely as Louis had foreseen.

Meanwhile Charles bestowed further honours on Barbara. On 3
August 1670, he created her Baroness Nonsuch of Nonsuch Park,
Surrey, Countess of Southampton and Duchess of Cleveland, with
remainder to her first and third sons, Charles and George Palmer.
The latter was described in the patent as the second son, which
was because the King still refused to acknowledge the paternity of
Henry.

The *Memoirs* of the Comte de Grammont describe a quarrel
which took place between Charles and Barbara during the course
of that summer. The King, though tolerant of most of Barbara's
infidelities, could not stomach Henry Jermyn and what Grammont
describes as *'plusieurs demêlés'* took place between Charles and his
former mistress. He teased her with wasting her money on Jermyn;
why did she not rather become the mistress of Jacob Hall, the
rope dancer? At this 'her impetuous nature flared up like a streak
of lightning' and she fairly flew at the King, accusing him of
baseness in reproaching her when he was content with women like
Frances Stewart, Winifred Wells and 'that actress baggage', by
which she meant Nell Gwynn. Barbara, of course, could not well
deny her affair with Jacob Hall, whom she had appointed to her

personal staff as a rope dancer at a wage of £5 per week.

The Comte de Grammont was called in to adjudicate between the King and Barbara, and his terms, which both parties accepted, were that she should forsake Henry Jermyn—who was banished from Court temporarily—and promise never to rail against Mistress Stewart or Mistress Wells again, while the King for his part could confer upon her the title of Duchess.[1] This, as we have seen, he duly did and Barbara found herself a peeress of England in addition to being an Irish Countess.

Having now attained this dignity, she sold Berkshire House and the greater part of its attendant extensive garden for building purposes; at the south-western corner of the estate she built for her own occupation a large red-brick mansion which was known as Cleveland House and there she resided for most of the rest of her time in England. On 23 February further grants came Barbara's way—the manor, hundred and advowson of Woking, the manor and advowson of Chobham, the manor of Bagshot (except the Park) and the advowson of Bisley, all in Surrey, as well as the hundred of Blackheath and Wootton.

In the course of 1672 Barbara had an affair with the playwright Wycherley, whose *Love in a Wood* pleased her so much that she attended two nights in succession. Determined to provoke an encounter with him, as she met his carriage in Pall Mall, she leant half her body out of hers and laughing loudly called, 'You, Wycherley, you are the son of a whore.' Recovering from his initial surprise the playwright made his coachman turn and pursue the Duchess and his speech of reply ended on such an ardent note that even the accomplished Barbara blushed. Though their consequent affair put Wycherley in some danger through the malevolence of Barbara's kinsman and enemy, the Duke of Buckingham, her interest eventually won him the favour of the King.[2]

Roger, meanwhile, was as usual considerate of his family's welfare. On 20 November he resettled the Dorney estates on the sons of his half-brother, Sir Philip, in tail male and thus it is that the present Palmer family of Dorney is descended from the children of Sir James by Martha Garrard and not those by Katherine Herbert.

Roger was also concerned regarding the education of his niece,

Phoebe. As long ago as 22 September 1668 he had written to her parents recommending that she should go to the Abbess of Pontoise, Lady Nevill. It seemed that this idea did not find favour with Sir Philip and Lady Phoebe, for on 15 April 1671 Roger wrote to Lady Palmer from Aachen:

'. . . As to Phoebe, what I proposed I did really believe would have been for her good, but since her father and you are of another opinion I hope you will consider my intention and believe that I have and ever shall have a concern for anybody that belongs to you, much more for so near a relative.'

Evidently Roger got his way, for in December 1671 the Blue Nuns' Diary recorded that 'In the month of December Mis Phoebe Palmer a Protestant was sent to us for education by the Earle of Castlemaine.' Equally evidently her parents had cause for concern, for a later entry reads:

'The first of Aprill 1672 Miss Phoebe Palmer niece to the Earle of Castlemaine made her abjuration of the Protestant religion and was received into the Communion of the Holy Mother of the Catholic Church by my Lord Abbot Montague.'[3]

This Abbot was a Benedictine who had become Grand Almoner to the Queen Dowager Henrietta Maria in 1665. He was not directly related to the famous Bishop Montague who, by odd coincidence, was a native of Dorney, albeit of the Vicarage and not of the Court.

Roger had succeeded in piloting Phoebe firmly into the arms of the Roman Church. His own daughter, Lady Anne, had however only spent a brief period in a French convent—to wit, the Monastery at Pontoise, where the Lady Nevill was Abbess. She arrived there some time in 1671 and returned to England in November 1672.

The Montague family lived at Boveney Court from at least the 15th century to the early 18th century and were substantial landowners and tenants in both Boveney and Dorney. One of them, the Reverend Lawrence Montague was Vicar of Dorney from 6 March 1572. His son Richard Montague, born in Dorney Vicarage round about the year 1578, educated at King's College, Cambridge, became Dean of Hereford in 1616 and then Canon of St. George's Windsor. His next step was Bishop of Chichester, whence he was translated to Norwich in 1638. He died in April

1641 and was buried in Norwich Cathedral: a High Churchman, he was far in advance of his time and advocated that Anglicans should regard the Roman Catholics as a true sister Church. In a book entitled *Apello Caesarim* he appealed to James I to support his opinions against the schismatics. Fuller said of his writings 'his great parts were attended with a tartness of writing: very sharp the nib of his pen, and much gall with his ink, against such as opposed him.' Charles I made Montague a Royal Chaplain and Archbishop Laud made great use of his scholarship. He had influence far beyond his century but perhaps it was fortunate for him that he did not live to see the Civil War.

On 1 August, Barbara's son Henry was married by the Archbishop of Canterbury to the five-year-old daughter of the Earl of Arlington, Isabella, in the presence of the King and of 'the grandees of the Court' as Evelyn relates. A fortnight later Henry was created Earl of Euston and Charlotte was granted the privileges of a Duke's daughter.

On 10 December 1672 the King granted arms to each of his three natural sons by Barbara—to Charles, Earl of Southampton, the arms of England differenced with a bend argent, to Henry, Earl of Euston (whom he now recognised) the same, but with a bend componée argent and azure and the third, Lord George Fitzroy, the same, with a bend componée ermine and azure. On 28 February 1673, it was Lady Anne's turn and that of her sister, Charlotte; they were each made a Lady Companion of the Order of the Garter, the knighthood of which had been conferred on their brothers Charles and George a month earlier.

Ten days after Anne's return, on 20 December 1672, Roger Jenyns dedicated to her a superb vellum book containing 'the pedigree of her ancient family and alliance.' It contained a full genealogical tree from the 14th century Palmers of Angmering, with the arms of each generation painted in colour and details of all the noble houses into which the Palmers had married. It is this same superb vellum book which, though additions have been made to bring it up to date, remains in the keeping of the Palmer family at Dorney. It contains portraits of almost three-dimensional likeness of Anne, Roger, Barbara and Anne's uncle, aunt, grandparents and great-grandparents.[3]

On their mother the King had conferred the palace and park of

Nonsuch in Surrey, of which she already bore the title, on 18 January 1671. Soon afterwards Barbara became possessed of a very fine and handsome lover, none other than her own second cousin once removed, John Churchill. He was now twenty-one years of age, an Ensign in the Guards and had just returned from service in Tangier, which had become a British possession as part of Catherine of Braganza's dowry; in his boyhood he had been a page in the household of the Duke of York. It was said that he was accidently introduced to Barbara by his aunt, a governess to the family and daughter of Sir John Drake of Ashe, Devon where Churchill was born. She was a distant relation of the great Sir Francis. Though nine years younger than Barbara, Ensign Churchill succumbed to her undoubted charms and remained her lover until his engagement to Sarah Jennings four years later. To Barbara's munificence towards him must be attributed the foundations of Churchill's wealth and perhaps his advancement in the army; she gave him 140,000 crowns out of her privy purse and obtained for him the post of Groom of the Bedchamber to the Duke of York. Great things have small beginnings, and it is interesting to consider that the career of the famous Duke of Marlborough was profoundly influenced by an affair with Barbara Palmer.

Possibly her taking him as a lover was not unconnected with the rising in the royal firmament of a new star in the shape of Louise de Keroualle, the lovely Bretonne before mentioned; Charles had first met her on her arrival at Dover in 1670, but it was a long time before she yielded to his desires. When at last she did and Charles created her Duchess of Portsmouth, suddenly her gentle humility deserted her and she became as imperious as Barbara, though far more ladylike with it than the latter's vitriolic temperament could ever allow her to be. Louise was 'baby-faced' with black hair; Barbara bold, with lovely auburn hair, a striking contrast; but Louis XIV, though he had engineered Louise into the English royal bed, did not contrive through her to influence English royal policy and he had the mortification of seeing Charles take Barbara's advice, not hers. Barbara 'in a manner took her leave of the King's bed, to make room for more preferred Rivals, and fresher Beauties', but the King was still wroth when he nearly surprised Churchill in Barbara's closet and the resourceful John

IX ANNE PALMER, COUNTESS OF SUSSEX
from the painting by Sir Godfrey Kneller in Dorney Court
(reproduced by courtesy of Lt. Col. P.D.S. Palmer; photograph by Michael Arthy)

PHŒBE, DAUGHTER OF SIR HENRY PALMER, AND
WIFE OF SIR PHILIP PALMER OF DORNEY.
BY JANSEN, 1632.

X LADY PHOEBE PALMER
wife of Sir Philip Palmer of Dorney, daughter of Sir Henry Palmer of Howletts;
from the painting by Janssen, 1632, now in Dorney Court
(reproduced by courtesy of Lt. Col. P.D.S. Palmer; photograph by Michael Arthy)

XI THE SEVEN EMINENT TURKS

paintings brought back by Roger Palmer, Earl of Castlemaine, from his embassy to Constantinople, 1668

(reproduced by courtesy of Lt. Col. P.D.S. Palmer; photograph by Michael Arthy)

XII THE PRESENT HEAD OF THE PALMER FAMILY
Lt. Col. P.D.S. Palmer, D.L., J.P., seen outside Dorney Court
(*photograph by courtesy of* The Windsor, Slough and Eton Express)

saved the day by leaping from the window twenty feet to the ground.

As Barbara's contemporary biographer describes it:

'Under the Circumstances not being able to brook so apparent a Slight, 'tis generally said she took a way to return the Kings inconstancy, which he had an opportunity afterwards to discover, for not having wholly laid aside his Amour there, one Day as he attended her a private visit, he found a certain Rival there, whom I think I need not name, for very few but must have heard of the story of Mr. Churchill being hid in her Closet. However, it did not happen ill for that Gentleman, for 'tis thought it very much hastened his Preferment, both by the Notice he took of him, and sending him Abroad into his Service, which was the first foundation of the great Glory he had since acquired.'[4]

VIII

HIGH TREASON?
(1673–1679)

ON 20 March 1673, the Test Act was passed which was to have very serious implications for Roger and his family. This prevented a Papist, unless he were an alien, from holding an office of profit or trust under the Crown and imposed penalties for various offences such as failing to attend Anglican services. Every person holding any office, civil or military, was required not only to take the Oath of Supremacy, but that he should receive the Sacrament in the form prescribed by the Church of England, or be incapable of receiving or retaining such office. A major reason for the introduction of the Act had been the public avowal, in 1671, by James, Duke of York, of his conversion to Catholicism—which had actually taken place clandestinely while he was in exile under the Commonwealth. Now he was one of the Test Act's first victims—one day Lord High Admiral, next day strolling unemployed and disgruntled in a London park. Barbara, having become a recusant, thus ceased to hold her office of Lady of the Bedchamber to the Queen—not that it mattered so much now that the King's passion for her had cooled.

Roger, fortunately for him, was still abroad, writing as always considerately about his family; from Brussels he wrote to Lady Palmer—

'I would advise in reference to Phil to urge my cousin Thomas Palmer to hearken out a place for him, yet (though he stays a little longer) if he minds his business, I know it will not be time lost but be very advantageous to him in making him thorough

56

paced in merchant accounts and writing a good hand. As for Charles, he is yet where I first directed him and there learns French and to write, nor do I intend to send for him from thence these 4 or 5 weeks yet till he has made a little further progress. After that I shall enquire some place in the Army to be ready against he shall be capable. I shall be very glad to hear of your being settled at Dorney according to your desires.'

In May 1673, Roger wrote again from Liège to Lady Palmer about various money matters:

'As for Phoebe, I will send your letter and one of my own also and when she finds no encouragement from any of us, she will do well I doubt not. Charles is well and will I hope be with me within this fortnight or 3 weeks and when I see him you shall hear further.'

Charles was Roger's nephew, born at Dorney in 1651 and ultimately destined to inherit the estate; 'Phil', referred to in the earlier letter, was his elder brother Philip, third son of Sir Philip Palmer by Lady Phoebe, his first wife.

On 11 August 1674, another of the same generation was the centre of a splendid occasion. Lady Anne, then aged thirteen and a half, was married at Hampton Court according to the rites of the Church of England by Dr. Crew, Bishop of Oxford, to Thomas Barrett Lennard, Lord Dacre, a Gentleman of the King's Bedchamber. There were present the King himself, the Duke of York, Prince Rupert, the Duke of Monmouth, the Earl of Arlington, Lord Danby, the Lord Treasurer, Lord Keeper Finch and the Earl of Suffolk, as well as the Spanish Ambassador. Windsor Herald recorded that

'About 9 in the morning the Lord Dacre was conducted to the Duchess of Cleveland's lodgings from his own by Mr. Anslow (Tutor to the Duchesses children), Sir John Baber and some other Gentlemen attending him, where the Bride was already drest to receive him. The King came from Windsor a little after Twelve a Clock and immediately repaired to the sd Duchesses Lodgings, and having staied a while, he led the Bride out in his hand, after them came the Bridegroome, then the Duke of York leading the Duchess of Cleveland, then Prince Rupert, then the Ladies of the kindred to the Bridegroome and Bride. In this manner they proceeded through the gallery, at the upper end whereof, in the Ante-Camera to the King's Bedchamber, they were married by Dr. Crew, the Bishop of Oxford, according to the Booke of Common Praier, half an hour after 12 o'clock.'

In all Barbara spent £2,943.1s.4d. on the wedding clothes with various London lacemen and milliners, and the King paid for a good half of this out of his secret service funds. A vast sum though this may seem for the 17th century, it must be remembered that, in addition to Anne's wedding, the same day the betrothal took place of her sister Charlotte, then aged ten, to the Earl of Lichfield, also a Gentleman of the King's Bedchamber. The Trustees of the Lady Anne received £20,000 as dower from the Exchequer and £18,000 was paid from the same source in July of that year to the Earl of Lichfield as dower for the Lady Charlotte. After her betrothal she remained with her mother for a few more years, whereas the Lady Anne took up residence at once at her husband's house in Warwick Street in the Parish of St. Martin-in-the-Fields. Later the same year he was created Earl of Sussex.

Barbara's other children were also thriving. On 15 September she and her third son, Lord George Fitzroy, arrived at Oxford in order to arrange with Dr. Fell, the Dean of Christ Church, for her eldest son, the Earl of Southampton, to enter the College. Young George was temporarily back at his birthplace, and Oxford must have brought back memories to Barbara of the events at Merton seven years before. On 1 October George was created Baron Pontefract, Viscount Falmouth and Earl of Northumberland. Nine days later, a grant of £6,000 from the revenues of the excise was made to George, Viscount Grandison, and Edward Villiers, Esq., Barbara's Trustees, for 99 years and the remainder to her son Charles and the heirs of his body; anything over was to go to Lord George Fitzroy and Henry, Earl of Euston and the heirs male of their bodies. On 21 October a further similar grant of £3,000 was made to each of Barbara's three sons and their heirs male. Thus did a King provide for his illegitimate progeny.

Roger, still abroad, had written to Lady Palmer on 20 April 1674 one of his typical family letters:

'As for Charles, though he costs three score pounds a year, I do not grudge it him, because he is improved as much as I can desire both in his inclination and other good qualities, and, I pray God his sister may do the like, who I must tell you spens me more than the £25 a year which her Father allotted her.'

Roger's namesake, the eldest son of Sir Philip Palmer by Lady Phoebe, died at the early age of thirty-one the next summer and was buried at Dorney on 9 July 1675, leaving a widow, the former Anne Ferrers, and a son, Philip, who was then the heir presumptive to the Dorney estates. Three months later James, brother of Roger Castlemaine and half-brother of the other Roger, was married at St. Martin-in-the-Fields to Katherine Southcote, a Lincolnshire lady. While these events might seem of minor importance, they were in fact to have direct bearing on the future history of the Palmers of Dorney, such are the twists of Fortune's wheel.

The following year Lady Anne, then aged fifteen and a half, gave birth to her first baby, who was christened Barbara after her grandmother; but almost immediately after her birth Anne separated from the Earl of Dacre and followed Barbara over to France.

The Blue Nuns recorded that Barbara had gone to live with them with her little daughter in 1675. In 1676 they wrote

'This year the Dutchess of Cleveland gave us fifty pounds. She also made great alterations in the hous as making a new staircase and changed the Reffectory and kitchen and wenscotting the Reffectory all which came to 280 Pistoles.'

Barbara had made a munificent gift of £1,000 to the Blue Nuns and in February her youngest daughter, Lady Barbara Fitzroy, 'came to be educated'. However, her mother's well-known tongue proved too sharp for some of her staff. In February 1677, Humphrey Prideaux wrote that

'Mr. Bernard, who went to France to attend on the two bastards of Cleveland hath been soe affronted and ill-used there by that insolent woman, that he had been forced to quit that employment and return.'

One of the said bastards, Henry, was created Duke of Grafton on 11 September 1675 and planned to marry the daughter of Lord Arlington. Barbara, however, did not approve; she had other ideas in mind, namely Lady Elizabeth Percy, daughter of the Earl of Northumberland.

That same year 1677, Barbara had received her last grant from the Crown, in the shape of the office of Chief Steward of the

Honour and Manor of Hampton Court. She had already made the best of her opportunities in France and was having an affair with the British Ambassador, the Hon. Ralph Montagu, a gay blade who had held the post for some ten years and who was described by Bishop Burnet as 'a man of pleasure'; but the following year the tables were turned on Barbara in the most unexpected fashion.

Barbara came to England in March, 1678, to use her influence with the King on behalf of Henry Savile and left Anne in the care of the Abbess of Conflans. On returning to Paris in May, Barbara discovered that her daughter had left of her own volition and gone to the Monastery of the Holy Sepulchre in the Rue Neuve de Belle Chasse, in the quartier St. Germain; she soon discovered why. On 28 May she wrote an angry letter to King Charles, complaining that Anne had left both her house and the monastery and was having an affair with the British Ambassador! Barbara did not admit in so many words that daughter had supplanted mother in Montagu's affections but she did admit that she herself had been having an affair with the Chevalier de Chatillon.

'I can hardly write this for crying'

she wrote

'to see that a child I doated on as I did her, should make so ill a return and join with the worst of men to ruin me. For sure never any malice was like the Embassador's, that onely because I would not answer to his love, and the importunities he made to me, was resolv'd to ruin me.'

She now besought the King to recall Anne to England to get her away from Montagu.

'I hope you will be just to what you said to me'

she reminded Charles

'which was at my own house, when you told me you had letters of mine; you said "Madam, all that I ask of you for your own sake is live for the future as to make the least noise you can and I care not whom you love." '

So typical a Carolean utterance was this that it has the undoubted ring of truth about it.

Charles's reaction was not exactly what Barbara wanted. He wrote to Anne, sternly commanding her to stay at the Abbey of Conflans, but this did not suit Barbara, who considered it too near her own residence. She promptly wrote back to the King suggesting that Anne be sent to the Abbey of Notre Dame de Port-Royal-les-Champs, at Magny-les-Hameaux near Versailles; her letter also disclosed that although Anne had been separated from her husband before her affair with the British Ambassador, she had now sent him a message asking him to have her back again. The affair reached a satisfactory conclusion when he did so and she bore him a daughter, also named Anne, in 1684.

Roger's travels had meanwhile taken him from Constantinople through Asia Minor, Syria, Palestine and along the North African coast, back into Europe and to practically every city of distinction in the west and so eventually back to Dorney. Unfortunately for him, however, Roger had returned at what was the very worst possible time, when Titus Oates was in full cry with his accusations of a Popish plot. Castlemaine was an ideal victim, known Papist that he was. On 24 October 1678 he was accused by Oates before the House of Commons of being a Jesuit priest, and of having, in Oates's hearing, wished success to the Popish plot.

Oates's testimonies had already sent enough unfortunates to a terrible traitor's death at Tyburn. Roger was not the sort of man to take false accusations lying down; he bided his time and prepared to defend himself. Oates declared that he had seen in the hands of Richard Strange, former Provincial of the Order of Jesus in England, a divorce from Barbara granted by the Papal Curia to Castlemaine. On the strength of this Roger was examined by justices of the peace, who evidently found there was a *prima facie* case made out and committed him in custody to the Tower on 31 October 1678.

On 23 January 1679 he was released on bail. No record exists of his having been formally charged, and we may suppose that there was insufficient evidence to prosecute him or to formulate a charge against him. While awaiting possible trial Roger boldly published an account of the sufferings of earlier victims, entitled: *The Compendium: or a Short View of the late Tryals in relation to the Present Plot against His Majesty and the Government.* Evidently undeterred from his scientific studies by the obvious danger he was in, he also published the same year The English Globe, being a stable and immobil one, *performing what ordinary Globes do and much more Invented and described by the Rt. Hon. the Earl of Castlemaine.*

As a result of further accusations by Oates, however, at the time of the so-called Mealtub Plot, he was committed to the Tower on 2 November 1679 on a charge of high treason.

IX

A PRINCE OF MANY VIRTUES
(1679–1685)

S O FAR as is known, all the Palmers of Wingham and Fairfield were staunch Protestants, as was also 64-year-old Sir Philip, head of the Dorney line, and his wife Anne. His surviving children, however, either had become or were soon to become recusants, probably due to Roger's influence, since it was a temporary phase lasting only some thirty-four years all told and may not have been unconnected with the impoverishment of the family and their dependence at that time on Roger for funds. Sir Philip's disastrous financial crash meant that his daughter Phoebe had no dowry and so became a nun, while the education of both Philip and Charles, the elder surviving sons, was largely at Roger's expense and instigation. He also naturally influenced his sister, Katherine and her husband, Marmaduke Dayrell and his younger brother James and sister-in-law, Katherine Southcote.

The first of the family to be presented by the Petty Constables for recusancy was Henry at the Easter Sessions, 1 May 1679, at Aylesbury. His cousin Marmaduke Dayrell was also presented. The Petty Constables of Dorney and Boveney were appointed annually at Sessions and held office for one year only.

Roger had been held in custody in the Tower since 2 November 1679. Four days after his committal Barbara had attended the wedding of her son, George, Duke of Grafton, at which occasion Evelyn recorded 'I staied supper, where his Majesty sate between the Dutchesse of Cleveland and the sweet Dutchesse the bride.[1] The Duchess of Grafton was in fact a renowned beauty, whose portrait was destined to be painted many times by such great

63

artists as Lely and Kneller.

On 16 June 1680, after seven months' incarceration, Roger was arraigned for high treason, and his trial before the Lord Chief Justice Scroggs began on 23 June. Scroggs had recently made a name for himself as a fearless judge, but his sympathies were obviously strongly anti-Papist, as he repeatedly interrupted Roger, and tried to browbeat him, as did Counsel for the prosecution. If ever the dice were loaded against a man, it was then, but Roger did not yield an inch. Coolly, competently and with signal skill and courage he defended himself, completely confounding the testimony of Titus Oates's gang of paid informers. The eventual result was that the Court, with grudging admiration, acquitted him.[2]

It was a difficult time to live. Although he had signed the Secret Treaty of Dover, the King had no intention of abiding by its terms; he was an avowed Protestant and despite a Catholic wife, and a leading Papist as his brother and heir, he succeeded in holding the balance between the conflicting interests with consummate skill, James, Duke of York, stubborn in his bigotry, was the root cause of much of the trouble: he sent his natural daughter by Arabella Churchill, Henrietta FitzJames, to the Blue Nuns to be educated in 1680, and despite the succession of 'plots' unearthed by Titus Oates the Catholic faction in England grew; both Houses determined to make an example of some prominent Papists. Of these attempts one of the most serious occurred in the early spring of 1681, when Parliament decided to inculpate Queen Catherine of Braganza. The old Earl of Stafford had been sent to the block as the result of a rigged trial in Westminster Hall; the same evidence was to be used to cause the downfall of the Queen.

The plotters in both Houses had reckoned without the King. On Monday, 28 March, he arrived at the meeting of Parliament in Oxford in a sedan chair with the curtains drawn close to hide his crown. He marched into the House of Lords alone, put on his crown and ordered Black Rod to summon the Commons before the Lords had recovered from their stupefaction; in astonishment the Commons came, to receive a severe homily from the King that 'proceedings begun so ill could end in no good.' With that he dissolved Parliament and without a further word stalked out, leaving both Houses speechless with amazement, walked to his waiting coach in which the Queen was sitting and drove straight with her to Windsor. Whatever might be laid at Charles's door by his enemies, none could say that he left his Queen unprotected at the mercy of his politicians.

Local witch-hunts spread to Wales, and for the first time, on 4 September 1682, James Palmer and his wife Katherine Southcote, of Buttington Hall, near Welshpool, were presented as recusants by the Court of Great Sessions.

Barbara had returned to France after the wedding of the Duke of Grafton in 1682 but apparently her visit to England had awakened in her a desire to come back. She must have sought and obtained Charles's permission to resume residence in England, for from a letter written by her to the Duke of Ormonde, dated 17 March 1684, it was evident that she had once more taken up her abode at Cleveland House.

Important events were deeply affecting the fortunes of the Palmers of Dorney. Roger, Sir Philip's eldest son, had died in 1675 and left his son Philip, then a minor, as heir to the Dorney estate; failing him, Henry, Sir Philip's second son, would inherit. Fate, however, now stepped in with another cruel disaster. About the year 1682, young Philip and his uncle Henry were bound for France in the Dover to Calais packet boat when, within sight of the latter port, the ship stranded in a gale and both were drowned.

In 1683 Sir Philip died, aged sixty-eight, and was buried in the family vault at Dorney. He left a widow, two unmarried sons, Philip and Charles, and one daughter, the nun Phoebe. So it was that Philip, a third son, inherited and became the third Palmer Lord of Dorney. He either was now or was soon to become a recusant and thus Dorney's first and only Catholic Lord.

James Palmer of Welshpool and his wife Katherine Southcote were presented again in both 1683 and 1684 for recusancy. These sporadic outbursts of arrests probably followed each Papist 'scare' and the latest may have been a backlash from the Rye House Plot. Katherine was a Catholic and so in her case it was not at all surprising. James died soon afterwards and now another curious quirk of Fate intervened in the Palmer fortunes; Katherine, the widow of one of the children of Sir James and Katherine Herbert—James being Roger's younger brother—married one of the older branch, descendants of Sir James and Martha Garrard, in the shape of Philip, the then lord of Dorney and thus for some years the lady of the manor was a Papist.

So 1684 drew to a close and with it the long reign of the 'Merry Monarch'. On 27 January 1685, having been received into the Roman church on his deathbed and having begged forgiveness of his heartbroken little Portuguese Queen for all the wrongs he had done her, Charles Stuart, epitome of royal charm, gaiety and licence, antithesis of severe Puritanisam, passed away. He left an aching wound in his country's heart, as Evelyn so well put it:

'Thus died King Charles II of a vigorous and robust constitution and in all appearance promising a long life. He was a prince of many virtues and many great imperfections; debonnaire, easy of access, not bloody nor cruel; his countenance fierce, his voice greate, proper of person, every motion became him; a lover of the sea and skilful in shipping; not affecting other studies, yet he had a laboratory, and knew of many empirical medicines, and the easier mechanical mathematics; he loved planting and building, and brought in a politer way of living, which pass'd to luxury and intolerable expense. He had a particular talent in telling a story, and facetious passages, of which he had innumerable; this made some buffoons and vitious wretches too presumptuous and familiar, not worthy the favour they abus'd; . . . He would doubtless have been an excellent prince, had he been less addicted to women who made him uneasy and allways in want to supply their unmeasurable profusion, to the detriment of many indigent persons who had signaly serv'd both him and his father. He frequently and easily chang'd favourites, to his great prejudice . . . certainly never had King more glorious opportunities to have made himself, his people and Europe happy . . . The history of his reigne will certainly be the most wonderfull for the variety of matter and accidents, above any extant in former ages; the sad tragical death of his father, his banishment and hardships, his miraculous restauration, conspiracies against him, parliaments, wars, plagues, fires, comets, revolutions abroad happening in his time, with a thousand other particulars. He was very kind to me, and very gracious upon all occasions, and therefore I cannot without ingratitude but deplore his loss, which for many respects as well as duty I do with all my soul.'[3]

This heartfelt epitaph by the calm diarist expressed the feelings of thousands. Few English Kings had been so adored, few with more reason; among those who most mourned his passing were the Palmers, consistent supporters of the Stuarts in fair weather and foul.

X

THE CATHOLIC KING'S
AMBASSADOR (1685–1688)

THE CHANGE which now came over England was profound. Charles may have sympathised covertly with the Catholic faith, made a secret treaty with Madame and been converted on his deathbed, but he never interfered with his subjects' Protestant beliefs. The new King, James II, proclaimed on 6 February, was of a different kidney, as fanatical as most converts are; though a first-rate admiral, he was a bigoted and blinkered monarch whose obstinacy led him in three short years to disaster.

At his coronation Barbara's son, the Duke of Grafton, performed the office of Lord High Constable. A few months later he was on a royal assignment of a different sort. Charles II's bastard son by Lucy Walters, James, Duke of Monmouth, claiming the throne as the rightful Protestant heir, had landed at Lyme Regis and made his way across West Dorset and Somerset to Taunton and Bridgwater, where he raised his standard. The Royalist forces under Lord Feversham—a courtier-figurehead, given the command because James distrusted the true commander, Lord Churchill, who, however, as deputy bore most of the responsibility—hastened to meet them and so, amid the rhines and withies of Sedgemoor, the bloody carnage ensued; but the Duke of Grafton, sent by Feversham in command of a detachment of foot guards to the hamlet of Norton St. Philip where the Duke of Monmouth lay, found himself almost cut off by the rebel horse and but for a lucky intervention of Feversham's mounted grenadiers would certainly have been killed.

That was the fate of Monmouth and his supporters, wretched, simple West country farm workers for the most part, whom the bloodthirsty Colonel Kirke and his 'Lambs' butchered on the battlefield and Judge Jeffreys in his Bloody Assize killed by judicial means, hanging, drawing and quartering hundreds, transporting and whipping hundreds of others. It was an example of metropolitan frightfulness designed to cow the West country into submission, and it is still remembered with hatred and loathing. The reaction elsewhere to the Rebellion was to close the ranks of the Catholics, and preferment came the way of many, not least Roger Castlemaine, whom James selected as his Ambassador to the Papal See. The prime object was to procure a cardinal's hat for the uncle of James's Queen, Mary of Modena. Roger embarked from Greenwich on 15 February 1686.

It might have been supposed that the man who had been such a successful Ambassador to a Moslem power on behalf of a nominally Protestant King would have been superb in a similar position on behalf of a Catholic King to the Supreme Pontiff. Nothing could in fact be further from the truth and one may wonder why Roger's embassy was so disastrous. Had the heady wine of seeing his religion ascendant in England, of being entrusted with this important mission on behalf of the man who would restore Catholicism as the state religion, gone to his head? Was it a vain streak in Roger's nature which was a fatal flaw in his character when given great responsibility? Was it the machinations of Papal politics which loaded the dice against him and made his embassy impossible from the start?

The answer to these apparent contradictions is to be found in the character and attitude of Pope Innocent XI, who has been described as the outstanding Pope of the 17th century in the matter of unswerving moral probity, a North Italian.

Innocent was engaged in a serious struggle with Louis XIV. He knew that the French King had plans for closer alliance with and aggrandizement of James II and was determined to rebuff them both. Roger's pressing the suit of Mary of Modena's uncle provided a good excuse to treat him with contempt; soon afterwards the Pope was able to complain about the conduct of the French Ambassador and then to block the candidature of Louis's nominee for the influential Archbishopric and Electorate of Cologne in the Holy Roman Empire. It is a cynical comment on human affairs that the two ardently Catholic Kings—the one who had dealt his country a body-blow by the Revocation of the Edict of Nantes and the suppression of the Huguenots, the other who in purblind fanatacism was cramming offices of State with Papists—should be the very men to displease their Church's Father in God. Yet so it was, and the rebukes administered to and complaints made about Roger were only reflections of a wider Papal policy.

On his way through France Roger paused at Paris and visited his nieces at the Convent of the Blue Nuns, who gratefully recorded that 'My Lord of Castlemaine gave ye house 480 livres'. On 13 April, Easter Sunday, he entered Rome and shortly afterwards presented his credentials to the Pope, Innocent XI. It was observed that 'His publick entry into Rome was pompously printed with a great many curious copper cuts, at King James the 2d's charge'. Roger wrote of

'setting up the armes of the Pope and His Majestie over his pallace with several devices of the Catholick religion triumphing over heresy and of the great splendour and magnificence of his reception.'

The reasons for his lack of success have been described in conflicting terms:

it was said that the Pope felt insulted because Castlemaine's title had only been granted to him so that his wife might become Charles's mistress. It was also said that Castlemaine, loyal to the interests of Queen Mary of Modena, importuned the Pope to such a degree that the latter had to avoid his insistence 'by a fit of coughing'. The Curia treated Roger scornfully, as it had many an ambassador before him, and after his recall to England the Pope sent a formal complaint to James II, who was constrained to apologise for his Ambassador's conduct. On his way back Roger called again at Paris where the Blue Nuns recorded,

'Received from My Lord of Castle Mayn then ambassador from Ye King of England James ye 2nd, to his holiness ye pope; for masses and prayers, 55 livres.'[2]

After his return home, on 26 August 1686, Roger made an indenture—'a jointure of £600 per annum for Dame Catherine Palmer accrued on her marriage—a portion for his niece Catherine of £4,100 from premises in Cardigan'.

Dame Katherine, widow of James, a younger son of Sir James Palmer by his second wife, married in about September 1686 Philip, the surviving eldest grandson of Sir James by his first wife. To begin with they lived at Buttington Hall near Welshpool, before moving to Llanfyllin. She was a Catholic who had been presented for recusancy in 1682, 1683 and 1684. Katherine the younger married Giles Chichester, of the great North Devon family of Arlington Court. Though it may seem strange that Roger was able to make such ample provision for his niece from revenues in Cardigan, it must be remembered that Castlemaine had inherited very extensive properties in Wales. He had Mivod, Poole and Buttington in the Welshpool area whence his mother hailed—a part of it held on lease from Christ Church, Oxford—some land at Clunn Park, Glamorgan, Mitchell Troy in Monmouth and a number of rectories in Cardigan; it was from these latter that he drew £1,000 per annum alone.

Nevertheless, while it behoved him to exhibit contrition and apologise for his ambassadors, James evidently did not consider Roger had failed. In fact, in 1687 he promoted him to his Privy Council—the highest attainment of his career—and in this we may see first a snub to the Pope and secondly the just reward for services rendered. Roger, who had made an unquestioned success of his embassy to the Porte, was not a newcomer to diplomacy and was certainly entitled to expect better treatment at the Pope's hands than he received. For with him and his royal master the behaviour of Innocent XI must have been a bitter disappointment.

As so often, for so many years, English success had been marred by the machinations of *Le Grand Monarque,* whose reign straddled those of Charles I, the Commonwealth, Charles II, James II, William and Mary, Anne and even one year of the House of Hanover—seventy-two years, an immense span of history in which to do damage. During the Stuart brothers' time there was an uneasy alliance—Charles generally getting the better of Louis by his brilliant tactics, while not seeming to do so, James feeling the brotherhood of religion while his policies were frustrated by those of Louis; but with the coming of the Protestant Succession this was the change to bitter conflict which was to sweep across the map of Europe.

In 1687 Roger granted the Blue Nuns his last recorded gift of six hundred livres. Also that year Barbara, by an indenture, granted the reversion of her two-thirds of the manor of Woking to her son the Duke of Grafton, now Vice-Admiral of England and in high favour with the King. In July he commanded a squadron of ships which conveyed the Queen of Portugal from Rotterdam to Lisbon. Meanwhile James continued to aggravate and alienate the vast majority of his subjects by sweeping Protestants out of office, replacing them with Catholics and finally bringing to trial Archbishop Sancroft of Canterbury and six other bishops for refusing to read from their pulpits the Declaration of Indulgence. The trial of the seven Bishops was the culminating point in the King's folly, and their acquittal was acclaimed with great public rejoicing. James, who had started so well, with even the Anglican clergy in a spirit of sweet reasonableness, was too bigoted and obstinate to realise that he was his own worst enemy. Despite his royal favour the Duke of Grafton became progressively more aligned against the King; secret ambassadors started to go back and forth to Holland as they had done a quarter of a century before, this time not to restore a King but to oust an existing one.

In the winter of 1687/8 Louis XIV founded the Court of St. Germain, at the old town of St. Germain-en-Laye to the west of Paris. Lady Anne Palmer joined it at its foundation and continued to be a member of it while she resided in France up to the death of her husband, Lord Dacre, in 1715. Her presence there was to provide a source of consolation to an exiled Queen all too soon.

It was very convenient for the plotters that William of Orange, Stadthouder of the Netherlands, was married to the Princess Mary, James II's elder daughter by Anne Hyde and, like her mother, a Protestant; thus by offering them the crown jointly the Stuart succession would not be broken and the Protestant faith yet preserved. Alas, for their plans on 10 June 1688, while troubled rumours were at their height, Queen Mary of Modena presented the King with an heir, who was christened James after his father; Roger Palmer was one of the signatories to the event, as was Queen Catherine of Braganza. This did not suit the Protestants' book at all, and a rumour was put about that the child was not the Queen's but had been smuggled into the Palace in a warming-pan. In any case it was the moment for action, and an invitation to

William to come to England was sent.

Wiser in his generation than Monmouth, he came with an army, instead of hoping to recruit one on arrival; like him he by-passed the south-east and made for the West country, but landed even further west, at Brixham in Devon, on 15 November 1688. Thence he made his way to Berry Pomeroy Castle, seat of a branch of the Somerset family and held his first 'Parliament' in the village; but he did not hurry, leaving the Devon gentry time to decide to join him, with the shadow of the Bloody Assize still hanging over them.

Two days after his landing the Duke of Grafton, with other lords spiritual and temporal, signed a petition to James II, asking him to call a Parliament; the previous day the Duke had in fact concocted a scheme with Lord Churchill to betray the King into the hands of the Prince of Orange. In the event, the plan misfired and the two, ostensibly at the head of royalist forces, rode westwards from Salisbury, not to stage another Sedgemoor but to offer their services to Dutch William. Thus sardonically Dame Fortune spun her wheel and the son and lover of Barbara, herself turned Papist, forsook the Catholic King and were foremost in bringing in the Protestant.[4] It was the only instance of Churchill's loyalty wavering in all his long career, and in his defence it must be said, as in the case of all true men who went over to Dutch William, that their care was for England and for the religion which their forebears had suffered so comparatively recently to maintain.

In December James II fled, taking the Great Seal with him and casting it into the Thames. He actually embarked on Christmas Day; Mary of Modena had preceded him and gone to St. Germain, where she appointed Lady Anne Palmer a Lady of her Bed-chamber. The Queen in fact treated her with signal honour; regarding her as the child of Charles II, not of Roger, she allowed her—an honour granted to only three other ladies—to be seated in the presence of French Princesses and Duchesses. So again Fortune smiled sardonically and while her brother betrayed the King, Anne was taken into the Queen's favour.

On the King's flight Roger Palmer, scenting bad times to come, withdrew to his estates in Montgomeryshire. So the brief summer of the Catholics' fortune was dimmed by the cold humours of a Dutch autumn and Barbara was destined to be sadly disappointed, despite her opportunism, while Roger was tumbled from his high diplomatic assignments once more into the grim embrace of the Tower of London.

XI

TO THE TOWER AGAIN
(1689–1702)

THE YEAR 1689 was vastly different from its immediate predecessors. On 13 February William of Orange was proclaimed King as William III, and on 11 April he and Mary were crowned. Barbara, seeing an opportunity to improve her fortunes despite the return of Protestantism, on 27 May placed Cleveland House at the disposal of the Dutch ambassadors sent by the States-General of Holland to congratulate William and Mary on their joint coronation. If she thought to endear herself to the royal couple by this manoeuvre, she had gravely misjudged the canny Prince of Orange and his devoted lady; indeed after their accession she found herself in financial straits, unable to obtain payment of the pension derived from the Post Office, which was now almost her sole source of funds. On 13 July she wrote to the Lords of the Treasury to complain, but her influence was gone; it was not until eight years later that payment began again together with the arrears and by that time she was in debt to the tune of £10,000.

Later that summer the House of Commons passed a Bill against Papists; one of its by-products was to embarrass the Queen-Dowager, Catherine of Braganza, by reducing the number of her servants so that she found herself forced to leave London and lodge with an apothecary in Islington. The blow fell with a vengeance for Roger Palmer; having gone to Montgomeryshire, he was arrested at Oswestry and sent to London where, on 28 October, he was impeached by the House of Commons for high treason in having gone to Rome as an ambassador, though how he could have refused when James II commanded him to go is not clear. The indictment accused him of 'endeavouring to reconcile this kingdom to the see of Rome.'

Once again he found himself committed to the Tower; once again the shadow of the scaffold fell over him—Tyburn, perhaps, with the monstrous brutality of hanging, drawing and quartering, or at best the headsman's axe on Tower Hill. The times were not propitious for Papists and anyone known to have enjoyed James's favour was suspect, a situation exacerbated by the old King's ill-advised invasion of Ireland from France. In the Tower when Roger arrived was the Earl of Arran, who had been committed at the end of February as a member of the opposition to King William; Evelyn had visited him there on 4 June.[1] He only remained a fortnight after Roger's arrival, however, as on 11 November he contrived to escape, and this event, too, was to have some significance for the Palmer family. Fortunately for Roger, his confinement did not last very long either; on 10 February 1690 he obtained his discharge on bail in his own surety of £10,000 and those of four friends of £5,000 each; but at the same time he was exempted from benefit of the Act of Indemnity. On 2 June he appeared before the Court of the King's Bench and was discharged.

The eagle eye of Queen Mary, regent in William's absence, was upon him, however, and as the Papist scare continued and the country braced itself for a French attack it is hardly surprising that Catholics at large were regarded as dangerous. On 30 June a great naval engagement took place off Beachy Head in which Barbara's son, the Duke of Grafton, Vice-Admiral of England, was reported to have borne himself with particular gallantry.[2] The Battle of the Boyne in Ireland gave added weight to the Protestants' fears; they had seen, only a few years ago, their luckless co-religionists in France, the Huguenots, fleeing as refugees to England, or, if unlucky, seized and sent to the galleys as slaves after the revocation of the Edict of Nantes. On 4 July Queen Mary issued a proclamation for the apprehension of Roger Palmer and others. He was seized again in August and conveyed to the Tower, but on 23 October petitioned to be either tried or bailed and eventually achieved the latter.

Things were not going too well for some other members of the Palmer family either. Twice the same year Philip Palmer and his wife Katherine were presented as Papist recusants by the Court of Great Sessions at Llanfyllin, Montgomery. In 1688 Charles Palmer, as a Catholic, would have had to resign his commission in the Army and he seems then to have retired to Boveney. For the first time in his life he was presented for recusancy by the Petty Constables at the Michaelmas Sessions at Chesham on 9 October 1690 and was indicted at the Epiphany Sessions at Aylesbury on 15 January 1691 for being absent from church. That was the end of the witch hunts at Dorney and Boveney. They in fact only occurred between May 1679 and January 1681 and from October 1690 to April 1693.

In Wales, Philip Palmer after his marriage to the Catholic Katherine had moved from Buttington Hall to Llanfyllin. He and his wife, and all their men and maid servants, were presented for recusancy at the Court of Great Sessions of Llanfyllin on 5 May and 18 September 1690 and on 2 October 1691. These were the only occasions that Philip was affected.

Barbara's son Henry, Duke of Grafton died of a wound in his side received ten days earlier at the siege of Cork. He had been described as a good sailor and soldier but of a rough, uncouth disposition, very different from that of his gentle, beautiful Duchess, who remained the reigning beauty of the Court throughout William III's reign, beloved of the wits, poets and portrait painters of the age. As to Barbara herself, now fifty years of age, a rumour was going about that she had again become pregnant, but although this was almost certainly unfounded she seemed to have bequeathed a certain *légèreté* to her daughters: Anne had had an affair with Montagu, and now the youngest, Barbara, who, although given the sobriquet 'Fitzroy', was almost certainly the progeny of Churchill, gave birth on 30 March 1691 at Cleveland House to a son, the father of whom was the Earl of Arran, now committed to the Tower for the second time.

Queen Mary was scandalized and made one of the conditions for Arran's release that Barbara should withdraw at once to the Continent. She was not allowed much time to recover from childbirth, even allowing for the difference in the French and English calendars, for the annals of the Blue Nuns for 2 April recorded her profession as Sister Bernadette;

'Mon nom du Monde est Barbe FitzRoy et en Religion

*Bernadette fille du Roy de la Grande Bretagne Charles II eme
j'ay fait profession dans le Couvent des Bénédictines Angloises
de Pontoise de l'annee 1691 le 2 de avril.'*[2]

Barbara had apparently been told by her mother that she was
Charles's child; certainly the Convent accepted her as such and the
name 'Fitzroy' is attached to hers in most documents. She never
returned to England, but died a Blue Nun.[3]

The following year a greater lady still went into exile; the
Dowager Queen Catherine of Braganza, rehabilitated after many
humiliations, sailed from Margate for Dieppe on 1 April 1692,
travelling *incognita* through France and Spain till at last a
triumphant welcome awaited her at the frontier of her native land,
where, after a period of great honour as Regent, she was
ultimately to die and be buried at the Monastery of the Jeronimos
at Belém, far from the tomb of her life's love in Westminster.

More misfortune befell Roger in 1691, when a curious charge
was brought against him. On 22 May at the Exchequer a trial took
place between him and the King

'for 4,000 li of plate, which he had of King James where he
went on his embassy to Rome; the Earls counsel insisted on a
privy seal from King James, which they produced in Court,
dated 8th December, 1688, whereby the plate was given him
for his own use; but the witnesses not being positive whether it
past the seal really before or after the abdication of the King,
gave £2500 damages, the value of the plate'

—so wrote Narcissus Luttrell.

It would seem that Philip must have divided his time between
Llanfyllin and Dorney. On 12 April 1692, he held a General
Meeting of the several freeholders, customary and other tenants of
the Manor of Dorney and Boveney at which the stints of Common
rights were resettled and the ancient and laudable customs,
bye-laws and orders of the Manor were brought up to date. Why
this should have been done at a general meeting and not at a
manor court is not known. In the next two years he held four
courts.

It had been customary for the common fields to be kept for
winter corn, summer corn and fallow. At the Court of 13 March
1693 it was agreed that it should be lawful for the arable lands to
be ploughed for three years together and the fourth year to lie

fallow. This revolutionary change in husbandry did not become general practice in England until many years later.

At this period the manor courts were responsible for the Thames flood banks. For instance,

> 'It is ordered that the Churchwardens of Dorney shall make a rate for the repairing the Thames bank amounting to fifty shillings which shall be equally based upon such lands as are dampnified by the waters breaking over the same. And it shall be lawful to dig stuff to repair the Thames bank by the bank side where it shall want.'

Now the unfortunate Roger again made the acquaintance of the Tower. Although he had gone abroad to France and Flanders after his earlier release, Queen Mary's writ of apprehension of 4 July 1690 still stood out against him, in spite of the fact that she herself had died from smallpox at Christmas, 1694. Roger had gone first to St. Germain in 1692 and in August, 1694, had stood godfather to three children born at the Court of James II. On 3 September 1695 a Bill of High Treason was issued against him and on 12 September 1695, he was summoned to attend the Irish Parliament in his capacity as Earl of Castlemaine and, failing to do so, on his return to England on 28 February 1696, he was duly arrested and committed to the Tower. Again no trial took place and on 18 July he was released on condition of going overseas again, to which he was nothing loath. After all, he had his niece Phoebe at Liège, in whose welfare he was deeply interested. In May he had contrived to send her fifteen crowns towards the expenses of a journey she had to make to Tongres. This was not so usual for a nun, but the records of Liège suggest that she had to consult a specialist or take the waters occasionally, for which she needed the permission not only of her own Abbess but of the ecclesiastical superiors as well. Professed nuns were allowed to leave their convents for short periods for health reasons and no doubt the journey to Tongres, some thirty miles on the Louvain side of Liège, was made for this purpose.

Some two years after Sir Philip had died we find that it was his widow, Dame Anne, who presented the Rev. Thomas Henning to the living of Dorney and not Philip, his son and heir. She herself must then have died because on 19 July 1698 the Reverend John Griffith was presented by King William III "by lapse". It seems very likely that the reason for this may have been that Philip, as a Catholic, could not be an acceptable patron. If this were indeed the case, then he must have immediately changed back to Protestant, because it was he who presented the Rev. William Dodd, inducted on 25 September 1699. In 1698 a new bell inscribed 'William Eldridge made mee' was hung in Dorney Church and we may suppose that this marked the occasion of Philip returning to the Protestant fold. His wife Katherine, however, remained a Catholic. It must have been about this time that his younger brother Charles also changed back to the Protestant faith.

Barbara had meanwhile been forced by lack of funds to leave Cleveland House and take up residence in Arlington Street. While there she continued her long-standing battle with the Lords of the Treasury to recover the Post Office pension granted her by Charles II, which had dried up on William's accession. Repeated appeals to William generally drew the reply that he had just gone abroad, or there was nothing in the Treasury, but eventually he was mollified to the extent that on 30 July the Lords of the Treasury wrote to the King's Secretary

> 'that His Majesty, having been pleased to say that when he gave directions for the Civil list, his Maty would be pleased to give order for the pencon of the Duchs of Cleveland, their Lo^ps being earnestly applied to by her Grace, who hath recd not payt for some time past, and appears to be in great want, and considering that her title to ye said pencon is secured by sevrall Acts of Parlt, their Lo^ps could do no less than to desire he would move the K. for his Matys direction concerning the said pencon.'

On 5 August the King agreed, desiring a payment to be made to the Duchess of Cleveland on the arrears of her pension proportionate to what had been paid to other great persons and on the 24th the Lords of the Treasury ordered the Postmaster-General

> 'to satisfy ye Dutchess of Clevelands warrt of £2,350 by 100 li a week for 23 weeks and 50 li the last week, the first payment to be made this week.'[4]

At last Barbara was solvent again, and the pension was paid for the rest of her life.

So the 17th century drew to a close. In September 1701, Louis

XIV recognised James II's son James, 'the Old Pretender', as King James III of England and Dutch William's announcement of this roused the English to fury. War was declared against France in 1702, but William died the same year and his sister-in-law Anne succeeded him.

THE LAST OF THE STUARTS
(-1689–1702)

O N THE death of Dutch William a very different person ascended the throne; the Princess Anne, kindly if not particularly talented, had for some years during Mary's lifetime been estranged from her sister and after her death William, though publicly reconciled, had never taken her into his confidence. Now, with her the star of John Churchill and his lady, Sarah Jennings, who for many years had been her confidante, her 'Mrs. Freeman' to Anne's 'Mrs. Morley', ascended too. But the star of the Palmers was waning and the great figures of the Stuart age were about to leave the stage.

Philip Palmer had made his will on 10 April 1700 and in it he had given instructions to be buried 'in my vault at Dorney aforesaid amongst my ancestors',[1] but in fact this did not take place when he died three years later; he was buried at Llanfyllin. Now suddenly his brother Charles, at the age of fifty-two, found himself most unexpectedly heir to the estate at Dorney. Of all the grandchildren of Sir James and Lady Martha Palmer, only two remained: Charles and his sister Phoebe, the nun of Liège—and Charles was still a bachelor. The only other person left to inherit would be Roger Castlemaine, survivor of Sir James's second marriage and he, too, had no heir, unless one counted Anne, Countess of Sussex, which was at best most uncertain. Charles therefore decided to marry and found himself a bride far younger than himself, his own distant relative Jane Jenyns or Jennings, daughter of John Jenys of Hayes, Middlesex. She was only sixteen and three-quarters when she married Charles there on 29

December 1705, and from their union sprang two sons and two daughters and thus the present Dorney line.

But before this marriage took place an older figure on the Dorney scene·had passed away, but not at Dorney. On 21 July of the same year Roger, Earl of Castlemaine, who had returned quietly from the Continent and was living at Philip's old house at Llanfyllin, died at Welshpool and was buried where the forebears of his mother lay. His Welsh estates had been almost his sole source of income for nearly fifty years and for him Dorney, despite his temporary lordship, was the property of his half-brother Philip and his issue. Hence Roger did not elect to be buried there. He had led a chequered life, had tasted the highest royal favour and the cruellest disgrace, had been infatuated but repudiated, courageous but impetuous.

His estranged wife waited only four months and then, on 25 November, she was married in her house in Bond Street to the famous dandy, Major-General 'Beau' or 'Handsome' Feilding. The ceremony was performed by Father Duarte, otherwise Father Remigius, chaplain to the Portuguese Ambassador, and the witnesses were Henry Eyre, a barrister of Gray's Inn, Michael Ross, a jeweller of Covent Garden, and Mrs. Anna Sackville, wife of Major-General Edward Sackville, a former Governor of Tangier. Sackville had been a strong adherent of James II both in England and during his exile at the Court of St. Germain. In addition, there were as witnesses Susanna Weldon and three of Barbara's servants.

'Beau' Feilding had lodgings in Pall Mall. He was the eldest son of George Feilding of Hillfield Hall, near Solihull in Warwickshire, and his mother was of the family of the Earl of Denbigh and a descendant of the Imperial House of Habsburg. Feilding, who was born in 1656 and had matriculated at Queen's, Cambridge, at the age of sixteen, had, as a young man, been in command of a regiment in the Imperial Army. Later he obtained a similar command in the English Army and achieved great favour with James II, who in 1685 made him a bounty of £500. Feilding always had an eye to the main chance and had married two heiresses, first the Hon. Mary Swift, daughter of Viscount Carlingford, and, after her death in 1682, the Lady Margaret de Burgh, daughter of Viscount Clanricarde. She died in 1698 and for seven years Feilding remained a widower gay; now he had hopes of

Barbara's supposed wealth but was by no means pleased with the allowance of £100 a week she made him from her revenues from the Post Office.

Worse was to come for Barbara, however, than Feilding's extravagence; for once in her life she, the mistress of great men had met her match. On 25 July 1706, she fled from Handsome Feilding, having discovered that his marriage to her was bigamous; on 19 November 1705, a matter of a few days before her wedding to him, he had married one Mary Wadsworth. On 6 December 1706, he was placed on trial at the Old Bailey and granted bail, which was renewed. Eventually, on 15 January 1707, he was convicted but was able to produce Queen Anne's warrant to suspend the sentence of burning in the hand which would normally have been his punishment. Barbara next instituted proceedings for annulment of the marriage in The Arches Court, where it was granted on 23 May, in the presence of her sons, grandsons and son-in-law.

Barbara was pronounced free to marry whom she wished, but the sands of time were running out for her and undoubtedly the great deception of which she had just been a victim told on her. She spent her last years in a house in Chiswick with her young grandson, Charles Hamilton, the son of her daughter Barbara Fitzroy and the Earl of Arran. This boy had already found much favour at the Court of St. Germain. So, while the country and the Continent rang to yet more in the series of Marlborough's great victories—Blenheim, Ramillies, Oudenaarde, Malplaquet—the life of his one-time mistress was drawing to a close. On 11 August 1709, Barbara, sensing the end approaching, made her Will; about the same time she fell ill of dropsy, which destroyed the remaining vestiges of her beauty and swelled her to a monstrous bulk. Mercifully it did not last long, and at her home in Chiswick, on 9 October, Barbara Villiers passed away at the age of almost sixty-nine.

After all the turmoil of her life and the scandals which attended her, we may find a reasoned epitaph in the words of a contemporary, who wrote the *Memoirs of the Life of Barbara, Duchess of Cleveland* in that same year, 1709:

> 'Whatever Character hath been given to this lady, rais'd to those
> Dignities she enjoyed by satisfying the Pleasures of a Prince,

which condition is alway attended with much Envy, we cannot but take notice, that her Birth and Quality were otherwise very noble; and the King might add to her Titles, but very little to her Blood; she was the daughter of William Villiers, Viscount Grandison in Ireland (though of a very Noble and Flourishing Family in England) and the Wife of Roger Palmer, Esq., who was created Earl of Castlemaine.'

The frontispiece to this book is an etching of her, the hair done in the becoming ringlets which were fashionable in her youth; she had been the subject of many paintings by great men, such as Lely and Kneller and to her startling beauty she added a brilliant wit, quick repartee and a devil-may-care boldness and daring which delighted many men and enslaved a King.

So Roger and Barbara, their long separation in life over, remained separate in death by close on a hundred leagues, his remains in a small town in the Marches of Wales, hers in an unadorned and unmarked grave in Chiswick, neither where we might perhaps have thought to find them, in Dorney. Of the great family of the days of Charles I and Charles II, few remained. Phoebe was still in her nunnery in Liège and destined, despite her indifferent health, to live on into the reign of George II. Katherine, widow of James and Philip, had gone to France after her second husband's death and entered a convent of Augustinian nuns. Charles Palmer was lord of Dorney, but he survived only a week after the death of Queen Anne on 1 August 1714 and thus, though his children by his young wife, the relative of the Queen's sometime confidante, remained, it could be truly said that the generations which had been such great supporters of the Stuarts died with them. There remained only Barbara's daughter, Lady Anne, Countess of Sussex, still at the Court of St. Germain, and her cousin, Katherine Chichester, far away in North Devon.

All Queen Anne's children had died, though the one in whom she pinned such hopes, the Duke of Gloucester, had survived till 1700. She had then agreed to the Act of Settlement, by which the English Crown was to pass to the descendants of her great aunt, Elizabeth, James I's daughter, in the person of George, the Elector of Hanover, who ascended the throne as George I. With him another dynasty and another age began for England, the Protestant succession firmly assured. The Palmers remained at

Dorney, but the age when they were so near the Throne, when they gave everything in the service of the House of Stuart, be it life, or wife or even a modest pineapple, was somehow over.

NOTES

Prologue
1. *Domesday Book,* Dorney, Bucks.
2. Ann. Theok., 78
3. Ann. Dunst., 235
4. Dugdale, *Monasticon,* VI, 545—6
5. *Records of Bucks,* 1779, Vol. V
6. *Montgomeryshire Collections,* Vol. LVIII, Part 2.
7. Palmer Pedigree
8. Chron. of A. Jane; Notes by Miss Jones
9. *ibid.*

I
1. Palmer Pedigree
2. The Liberty of Boveney was part of the ecclesiastical Parish of Burnham. In August 1642 the Rev. Edward Hawtrey was presented to the living of Burnham by his wife, Margaret, widow of the Rev. John Wright. The presentation was vested in him in 1644. He was ejected during the Civil War and one Benjamin Perkins intruded, but he in turn was ejected in 1661 and Hawtrey reinstated. He died on 29 October 1669; his son, the Rev. John Hawtrey, Fellow of Eton College, on 28 October 1681 granted the advowson to Eton College. The Chapel of St. Mary Magdalene, Boveney, became a chapel of ease of Burnham. By an Order-in-Council dated 25 May 1911 Boveney Liberty was ecclesiastically annexed to Eton, to which Church St. Mary Magdalene became a Chapel of ease.
3. Chamberlayne, *Angliae Notitiae*

II
1. *Mont. Coll.* op. cit.
2. *VCH,* Bucks, iii, 223
3. Steinman Steinman, 7 (cf. Boyer. f.48)

4.   *ibid.* 13 (cf. Letters of Philip, Ld. Chesterfield, F. 91)

III
1.   Cf. Prince's Worthies of Devon

IV
1.   Pepys, 17.1.1660
2.   *ibid.*
3.   *ibid.* 16.3.1660
4.   *ibid.*
5.   *ibid.*
6.   *ibid.* 25.4.1660
7.   *ibid.* 3.5.1660
8.   *ibid.* 13.5.1660
9.   *Letters of King Charles II*

V
1.   Pepys, 13.7.1660
2.   *ibid.* 20.4.1661
3.   *ibid.* 7.12.1660. The title 'Limerick' had been held by Barbara's grandfather.
4.   *ibid.* 30.6.1661
5.   *ibid.* 10.11.1661
6.   *ibid.* 7.5.1662
7.   *ibid.*
8.   *ibid.*
9.   *ibid.* 21.5.1662
10. *ibid.* 31.5.1662
11. *ibid.*
12. *Letters of King Charles II*
13. *ibid.*
14. Pepys, 6.6.1662
15. *ibid.* 16.6.1662
16. *Letters of King Charles II*
17. Pepys
18. *ibid.*
19. Steinman, p. 60
20. Pepys, 1.1.1663
21. *ibid.* 3.1.1663
22. *ibid.* 1.3.1663
23. *ibid.* 13.7.1663
24. *ibid.* 3.7.1663

VI
1.   Pepys, 14.9.1662
2.   Steinman, p. 63

3. Evelyn, 9.8.1662

A great deal of controversy still centres round the pineapple story. On the high table in the great hall of Dorney Court stands a model pineapple carved in stone with a plaque bearing the inscription 'Made to commemorate the fact that the first pineapple grown in England was cultivated at Dorney Court by Rose, gardener to Sir Philip Palmer, Kt. The original picture of King Charles accepting the pineapple is now at Ham House, C.1665.'

On the back of the Ham House painting, which hangs in the Marble Dining Room, is an inscription reading 'Charles 2d and Rose his gardiner, presenting to him the first Ananas raised in England.' The inscription continues that it was copied by Thomas Stewart or Hewart, aged 20, 'in October, 1787, from the original by Danckers in the collection of Mr. Walpole at Strawberry Hill.'

The artist referred to is the Flemish Henry Danckaerts, who came to England in 1668. At a banquet on August 19 of that year Charles II gave Evelyn 'a piece of that rare fruit the King Pine, growing in Barbados and the West Indies; the first of them I have ever seen.' He saw the Queen Pine, as we have noted, in 1661.

Much play has been made (by those who would decry the Dorney legend) of the fact that the house depicted in the background of Danckaerts's painting is certainly not Dorney Court. It is generally accepted, however, that Danckaerts painted the picture abroad, and what more likely than that he should have painted an imaginary house in the Dutch style, which the house in the picture with its formal gardens much resembles.

Horace Walpole wrote in 1780 to the Rev. William Cole regarding the picture. In the O.U.P. edition of his *Letters* of 1904, Mrs. Paget Toynbee wrote that in the notice of the picture in the description of Strawberry Hill, Walpole conjectured that the house represented was Dorney Court, near Windsor. Bray's 1818 edition of Evelyn's *Memoirs* has a note regarding the entry of 9.8.1661: 'The scene of the presentation was Dorney Court, the seat of the celebrated Duchess of Cleveland.'

In an engraving of Danckaerts's painting made by Robert Grave in 1823 is an inscription: 'this plate of King Charles II receiving the first Pine Apple cultivated in England from Rose, the gardener at Dorney Court, Bucks, the seat of the Duchess of Cleveland.'

Correspondence on this subject appeared in *Country Life* as recently as 1959, including an article by Miles Hadfield on 14 May 1959 regarding the cultivation of pineapples in England.

The tradition of the Dorney pineapple has certainly been in the Palmer family for 300 years. It may not be irrelevant to note that there is a field in Dorney not far from the garden known locally as the 'Pin Garden'.

4. Pepys, 1.12.1666

5. Palmer Pedigree
6. Evelyn, 4.2.1668
7. *Poor Whores' Petition.*
8. *Memoir of Barbara,* I
9. Pepys, 4.4.1669

VII

1. Grammont, ii, 205/6
2. Steinman, 134/5
3. Palmer Pedigree. Some note of the French and Belgian convents to which the Palmers' and Barbara's children went may be useful. The *Blue Nuns,* so called from the colour of their ceremonial cloaks, were an offshoot of the English community at Nieupoort in Flanders which broke up, due to extreme poverty, in 1658. Their Order was the *Immaculate Conception of Our Blessed Lady;* in 1660 they took possession of a building in the Faubourg St. Antoine, then a respectable residential area on the left bank of the Seine in Paris. The convent was one of several religious properties in this stretch of open country in the St. Germain district, between the Bastille and the river. It possessed quite a large garden and a small wood. The Blue Nuns remained there until driven out in 1794 by the French Revolutionaires. A small part of their buildings still remains in the present Rue Charenton, a narrow street in a built-up area of Paris.

   The first Abbess of the Blue Nuns was Elizabeth Timperley until 1681, when she was succeeded by Lady Neville, daughter of Lord Abergavenny, who until that date had been Abbess of Pontoise in Normandy. The Blue Nuns' *Diary* from 1660 to 1680 was transcribed and edited by Susanna Hawkins, who had joined the Order in 1660 at the age of sixteen. From 1681 onwards it was kept up by Lady Neville. The *Diary* was edited and published as Volume VIII of the Catholic Record Society in 1910. The connections with the family were
   (a) *during Elizabeth Timperley's time:*

   10 January 1667
   Jane Darril, aged 7, and Barbara Darril, aged 6, arrived. They remained Blue Nuns until they died—Barbara of smallpox in 1699 and Jane in 1739.

   15 April 1671
   Roger wrote to Sir Philip and Lady Phoebe Palmer regarding his proposal that Phoebe should go to the Blue Nuns.

   December 1671
   Phoebe was sent to the Blue Nuns 'for education by the Earle of Castlemaine'.

   1 April 1672
   Phoebe abjured the Protestant faith and became a Roman Catholic.

2/12 May 1673
Roger's letters concerning Phoebe.

2 April 1674
Roger's letter regarding the expense of maintaining Phoebe.

25 April 1675
Phoebe leaves the Blue Nuns for Liège.

Last entry 1675
The Duchess of Castlemaine and her daughter Barbara Fitzroy
came to live there.

1676
The Duchess of Cleveland gave £50 plus alterations to buildings
costing 280 pistoles.

February 1677
Lady Barbara Fitzroy came to be educated. The Duchess of
Cleveland gave £1,000.

1679
The Duchess of Cleveland gave a silver lamp as a New Year's gift.

1680
Henrietta Fitzjames, natural daughter of James II and Arabella
Churchill, came to the Blue Nuns school.

(b) during Lady Neville's time

1681
Lady Neville became Abbess.

1682
The Duchess of Cleveland gave a great cloak and a silver chaffer
dish.

1685
Roger gave £10

1686
Roger gave 480 livres plus 55 livres for masses.

1687
Roger gave 600 livres.

22 November 1689
Lady Barbara Fitzroy clothed.

30 March 1691
Lady Barbara had a son by the Earl of Arran at Cleveland House.

April 1691
(12 April English calendar) Lady Barbara professed.

16 April 1689
Lady Henrietta Fitzjames clothed.

20 April 1690
Lady Henrietta Fitzjames professed.

27 August 1721
Lady Barbara Fitzroy left to become Prioress of the Royal Priory of St. Nicholas at Pontoise.

Monastery at Conflans (between Versailles and St. Germain-en-Laye)

March 1678
While Barbara was in England until May she left her daughter Anne there but Anne moved without permission to the *Convent of the Holy Sepulchre,* Rue Neuve de Belle Chasse, in the Quartier Saint-Germain.

June 1678
The King ordered Anne to return to *Conflans.* Barbara, however, suggested to the King that she should go to the *Monastery of Port Royal,* the celebrated Abbey of Port-Royal-des-Champs near Magny-les-Hameaux, between Versailles and Chevreuse. This was closed in 1679.

Monastery at Chaillot near Paris (founded by Queen Henrietta Maria for Nuns of the Visitation of St. Mary)

1668–9
Lady Anne Palmer there.

Monastery at Pontoise in Normandy
Pontoise lies north-west of Paris: Saint Louis's favourite palace was situated there. Lady Neville was Abbess there up to 1681.

12/22 September 1668
Roger recommended that Phoebe should be sent there at £30 p.a. until she was fit for marriage.
Katherine Darrell was already there.

1671–November 1672
Lady Anne Palmer there 'to be bred'.

Royal Priory of St. Nicholas at Pontoise

27 August 1721
Lady Barbara Fitzroy, having left the Blue Nuns, became Prioress there.

6 May 1731
Lady Barbara died there

Paris Convent of Augustinian Nuns

9th February 1730
Katherine, widow of Philip Palmer, died there.

Liège

25 April 1675
Phoebe left the Blue Nuns and arrived at Liège. F.800 received from Roger.

12 May 1676
Phoebe admitted to the Chapter

30 May 1676
Phoebe took the first habit (i.e. became a postulant)
Roger was to pay £150 plus £50 for clothing plus £20 per annum.

29 September 1676
Phoebe clothed (i.e. became a novice)

30 September 1677
Phoebe professed.
Roger gave £10 for her chamber.

1695
Phoebe contributed £14 towards the expenses of the Abbess's illness and pension.

May 1696
Roger gave Phoebe 15 crown towards the expenses of her journey to Tongres.

19 July 1741
Phoebe died there.

4. *Memoirs of Barbara,* 2.

VIII
1. Steinman, addenda I, p. 6
2. *ibid.* 148/9
3. Steinman, 149
4. *ibid.* 150
5. *ibid.* 156 ff.
6. Palmer Pedigree

IX
1. Evelyn, 6.11.1679
2. Tryal of Roger Palmer
3. Evelyn, 4.2.1685

X
1. Duke of Grafton 33/35
2. Cath. Rec. Soc *Miscellanea*
3. Steinman, 187
4. Duke of Grafton, 67

XI
1. Evelyn, 4.6.1689
2. Steinman, 188, quoting letter from Queen Mary to King William, 6.7.1690
3. Steinman, 189
4.

XII
1. *Montgomeryshire Collections.*
2. *ibid.*, Palmer Pedigree, Steinman 207, Boyer f.39
3. Steinman, 214 ff.
4. *ibid.*, 215/6 and Evidence
5. *Memoirs*

BIBLIOGRAPHY

Annales Monastici	5 vols. ed. H.R. Luard (Rolls Series, London, 1864–9) especially *Annales prioratus de Dunstaplia* in Vol. III *Annales monasterii de Theokesberia* in Vol. I
BOYER, Abel	*The History of the Reign of Queen Anne* (Roper, London 1703–18)
BRYANT, Sir Arthur	(ed) *The Letters of King Charles II* (Cassell, 1968)
BRYANT, Sir Arthur	*King Charles II* (Collins, 1931)
BURKE, Sir Bernard	*Dormant and Extinct Peerages* (Harrison, London, 1866)
BURKE, Sir Bernard	*The Royal Families of England, Scotland & Wales* (Harrison, 1876)
BURNET, Gilbert Bishop of Salisbury	*Bishop Burnet's History of his own time* (ed. Sir T. Burnet–Ward, 1724–34)
CARTWRIGHT, Julia	*Madame* (Seeley, London, 1894)
CATHOLIC RECORD SOCIETY	*Miscellanea* (Vol. x. 1915)
CHURCHILL, Sir Winston	*Marlborough: His Life and Times*
CRESSWELL, Madame and Damaris Page	*The Poor Whores' Petition* (1668)
DAVIDSON, Lillias Campbell	*Catherine of Braganza* (Murray, 1908)
DRYDEN, John	*Poems* (ed. J. Kirsley, 1958)
DUCHESS OF CLEVELAND's MEMORIAL	(1707)
DUCHESS OF CLEVELAND's	*Gracious Answer to the Poor Whores' Petition* (1668)
English Historical Documents	*1660–1714 (ed. A. Browning, 1953)*
Evidence	The Duchess of Cleveland's against Maj. Gen. Feilding (1705)
EVELYN, John	*Diary* (Ed. E.S. De Beer, O.U.P. 1955)
FARMER, D.L.	*Britain under the Stuarts* (Bell, 1965)
FITZROY, Almeric	*Henry, Duke of Grafton* (Christophers, London, 1921)
GARDINER, Dorothy	*The Oxendon Letters* (Constable, 1923)
GRAMMONT, Comte de (Count Hamilton)	*Memoirs* (ed. by Sir Walter Scott, Sonnenschein, London 1891)
GUMBLE, Thomas	*Life of General Monck, Duke of Albemarle* (London, 1671)

HARTMANN, C.H. — *Charles II and Madame* (Heinemann, 1934)

JAMESON, Mrs. — *Memoirs of the Beauties of the Court of King Charles the Second* (Colburn, London, 1838)

JANE, Queen — *Chronicle of and Two Years of Queen Mary*—by a resident of the Town of London (Camden Society, London, 1850)

JESSE, John Heneage — *Memoirs of the Court of England during the Reign of the Stuarts* (Bohm, 1857)

JONES, Anne — *Notes on Sir Thomas Palmer* (Trinity Coll. Dublin, 1959)

LOWER, Sir William — *Voyage of Charles II* (1660)

LUTTRELL, Narcissus — *A Brief Historical Relation of State of Affairs from September 1678 to April 1714* (O.U.P. 1857)

Montgomeryshire Collections — (Transactions of the Powys-Land Club) Vol. LVIII Pt. II (reprinted 1966)

MORESHEAD, Sir Owen — *Windsor Castle* (Pharoon Press, 1951)

MORRAH, Patrick — *The Year of Restoration* (Chatto & Windus, 1960)

PALMER, Roger in — *Dictionary of National Biography*

POTE, Joseph — *History and Antiquities of Windsor* (Eton College, 1749)

RECORDS OF BUCKS — 1779 Vol. V and 1903 Vol. VIII (Fraine, Aylesbury)

RERESBY, Sir John — *Memoirs* (London, 1734)

ROUVROY, Louis de (SAINT-SIMON) — *Memoires* (Blackie, 1901 etc.)

SANDWICH, Earl of — *Journal of Edward Montagu, Earl of Sandwich, Admiral and General at sea* (ed. R.C. Anderson; Navy Record Society, vol. 64, 1929)

SERGEANT, P.W. — *My Lady Castlemaine* (Hutchinson, 1912)

SKINNER, Thomas — *Life of General Monck, Duke of Albemarle* (1724)

STEINMAN, G. Steinman — *A memoir of Barbara, Duchess of Cleveland* (privately, 1871)

TIGHE & DAVIES — *Annals of Windsor* (Longmans, 1858)

Tryal of Roger Palmer, Earl of Castlemaine — before the Court of King's Bench (1681)

TURNER, F.G.
Victoria County History
VILLIERS, Barbara *in*

James II (Eyre & Spottiswode, 1948)
Buckinghamshire
Dictionary of National Biography

(In addition, I have had access to numerous family papers of Lt. Col. P.D.S. Palmer of Dorney Court and in particular the PALMER PEDIGREE, or VELLUM BOOK, presented to Lady Anne Palmer by Ralph Jenyns in 1672)

INDEX